W9-BLJ-843

GERMANY

ABDO
Publishing Company

GERMANY

by Susan E. Hamen

Content Consultant

Stephen A. Schuker

Professor, University of Virginia, Department of History

CREDITS

Published by ABDO Publishing Company, 8000 West 78th Street, Edina, Minnesota 55439. Copyright © 2012 by Abdo Consulting Group, Inc. International copyrights reserved in all countries. No part of this book may be reproduced in any form without written permission from the publisher. The Essential Library™ is a trademark and logo of ABDO Publishing Company.

Printed in the United States of America,
North Mankato, Minnesota
062011
092011

♻ THIS BOOK CONTAINS AT LEAST 10% RECYCLED MATERIALS.

Editor: Melissa York
Copy Editor: Susan M. Freese
Design and production: Emily Love

About the Author: Susan E. Hamen is a full-time editor of German heritage who finds her most rewarding career experiences to be writing children's books. She has written educational books on a variety of topics, including the Wright brothers, the Lewis and Clark expedition, the Industrial Revolution, and Pearl Harbor. She has toured Germany twice so far.

Library of Congress Cataloging-in-Publication Data
Hamen, Susan E.
  Germany / by Susan E. Hamen.
    p. cm. -- (Countries of the world)
  Includes bibliographical references and index.
  ISBN 978-1-61783-110-2
  1. Germany--Juvenile literature. I. Title.
  DD17.H33 2011
  943--dc23
                                         2011020916

Cover: Neuschwanstein Castle, Bavaria, Germany

TABLE OF CONTENTS

CHAPTER 1	A Visit to Germany	6
	Map: Political Boundaries of Germany	9
	Snapshot	15
CHAPTER 2	Geography: Scenic Beauty	16
	Map: Geography of Germany	20
	Map: Climate of Germany	27
CHAPTER 3	Animals and Nature: Creatures of the Forest	28
CHAPTER 4	History: An Imperial Past	42
CHAPTER 5	People: National Pride	66
	Map: Population Density of Germany	68
CHAPTER 6	Culture: A Classical Tradition	76
CHAPTER 7	Politics: Achieving Unity	94
CHAPTER 8	Economics: Industrial Leader	104
	Map: Resources of Germany	109
CHAPTER 9	Germany Today	116
TIMELINE		128
FACTS AT YOUR FINGERTIPS		130
GLOSSARY		134
ADDITIONAL RESOURCES		136
SOURCE NOTES		138
INDEX		142
PHOTO CREDITS		144

CHAPTER 1

A VISIT TO GERMANY

As you walk through the streets of Munich's old town, people bustle around you. Shoppers, sightseers, businesspeople, and shopkeepers all make their way across the city's famous Marienplatz, a square situated in front of the Neues Rathaus, or "new city hall." The shopping areas—particularly Neuhauserstrasse and Kaufingerstrasse—offer international names and designer brands, while the boutiques on Maximilianstrasse peddle more traditional German wares. You stop to browse the lederhosen, cuckoo clocks, steins, and Nymphenburg porcelain. Enticing smells from local bakeries and chocolate shops drift by. Mmmm! Your stomach begins to rumble. An early lunch is in order!

Continuing your walk, you spy the world-famous Hofbräuhaus beer hall. You stop inside and settle down at a long wooden table for a plate of Wiener schnitzel. While you wait, you join the other merrymakers in singing along with the Bavarian-style oompah band. The friendliness of the other patrons brings a smile to your face.

Marienplatz in Munich

1972 OLYMPIC SUMMER GAMES

In the summer of 1972, Munich hosted the Olympic Summer Games. The Olympic Park built in the city was revolutionary in its modern design and quickly became a Munich landmark. US swimmer Mark Spitz took home seven gold medals in the games, setting a record for the number of gold medals won in a single Olympics.

The 1972 Olympics marked the first time the games had been held in Germany since 1936, when the country was under Nazi control. In 1972, Munich was part of West Germany, and the West German government hoped to showcase a modern, democratic Germany. Sadly, the games were marred by a bloody terrorist attack that would become known as "The Munich Massacre." On September 5, eight Palestinian terrorists broke into the Olympic Village, killed two Israeli athletes, and took hostage nine Israeli athletes, coaches, and officials.[1] After a lengthy standoff with authorities, the terrorists and hostages were flown by helicopter to a military airport. There, German authorities attempted a rescue, but all of the Israeli hostages were shot and killed. All but three of the Palestinian terrorists were also killed, along with a West German police officer. Despite the horrific tragedy, the Olympic Games resumed a day later.

As noon approaches, people congregate in the Marienplatz to see the city's famous Glockenspiel on the front of the Rathaus. You listen to the bells chime and watch the life-size figurines dance in a circle. Like the other people in the square, you're captivated by the display.

Next, you walk a short distance to the Frauenkirche, or Cathedral of Our Dear Lady. Construction began on this Gothic-style cathedral in 1468. It's a landmark in Munich and a symbol of the Bavarian state capital. More than half a millennium of history surrounds you as you look up in awe at the soaring columns, arches, and stained glass windows.

Political Boundaries of Germany

You soak in as much of historic Munich as possible on your last day in the city.

INTO THE ALPS

Your brief stay in Munich gave you the perfect chance to indulge in some of the country's famous fare and to glimpse some of Germany's architectural history. As you check the departure schedule at the Munich central train station, you eagerly anticipate the next stop on your journey through Germany. You have just enough time to stop at one of the many food vendors and buy a chewy Bavarian pretzel to eat during the two-hour ride south to the foot of the Alps.

You've never seen the famous European mountain chain before. Will it be as magnificent in real life as in the pictures you've seen? Will the people in the south of Germany be as friendly and helpful as the ones you've encountered thus far? You board the train, find your seat, and settle in with your snack.

Before you know it, you've arrived at your destination: Füssen. Grabbing your backpack, you disembark. As you step off the train, the smell of pine trees and clean water enchants you. Standing at the little train station in the small town at the foot of the Alps, you see small

Germans play the alpenhorn during a festival in Füssen.

shops and restaurants lining the quaint cobblestone streets. Houses dating back to the Middle Ages remind you of the area's extensive history.

Ready to stretch your legs after the train ride, you set out on the 1.8-mile (3-km) walk to one of the world's most famous castles. You find the view of towering pine trees a sight to behold. You catch sight of Schloss Neuschwanstein, or "Neuschwanstein Castle," set against the backdrop of the Bavarian Alps. The majestic white castle rises up out of the foothills like a dream. You purchase your ticket in the tiny village below the castle and await your tour of this fairy-tale place.

SCHLOSS NEUSCHWANSTEIN

Neuschwanstein Castle is one of the most popular tourist attractions in Europe, and it also served as the inspiration for Disney's Sleeping Beauty castle. The name *Neuschwanstein* translates to "New Swan Stone." King Ludwig II of Bavaria built this fairy-tale castle across the valley from his father's castle, Schloss Hohenschwangau, and the foundation was laid in September 1869. The castle was intended to be a retreat in the rugged foothills and a tribute to famous German composer Richard Wagner. Detailed paintings depicting Wagner's operas adorn the walls throughout the castle. Ludwig moved into the still-unfinished castle in 1884 but lived there for less than a year before his death.

Neuschwanstein Castle

A COUNTRY DIVIDED

Following defeat in World War II (1939–1945), Germany was split into four zones, each occupied by one of the four Allied powers: France, the Soviet Union, the United Kingdom, and the United States. The intention was that each country would help to reestablish its war-torn portion of Germany. While France, the United Kingdom, and the United States worked to create democratic governments within their zones, the Soviet Union formed a Communist government within the zone it occupied. Relations between the first three zones and the Communist-controlled Soviet zone soon crumbled. In 1949, Germany was officially divided into two countries: the German Democratic Republic (or East Germany, as it was informally called) and the Federal Republic of Germany (or West Germany). The nation remained divided until 1989, when protests against the Communist government led to the overthrow of the East German government. East and West were reunited and Germany was once again one country on October 3, 1990.

AFTER THE WARS

Although Germany today is rich in history and offers countless opportunities for people in search of shopping, sightseeing, and athletic adventure, it has struggled to overcome a dark past. Many parts of the country were devastated during World War II (1939–1945), and remnants of that devastation are still evident today. In fact, Germany was split after World War II, forming East Germany and West Germany, and the two weren't officially reunited as one country until 1990. Today, Germany is dedicated to preserving its traditions and culture while allowing examples of its troubled past to serve as a reminder of the devastation of war.

SNAPSHOT

Official name: Federal Republic of Germany (in German, Bundesrepublik Deutschland)

Capital city: Berlin

Form of government: federal republic

Title of leader: president

Currency: euro

Population (July 2011 est.): 81,471,834
World rank: 16

Size: 137,847 square miles (357,022 sq km)
World rank: 62

Language: German

Official religion: none

Per capita GDP (2010, US dollars): $35,900
World rank: 31

CHAPTER 2
GEOGRAPHY: SCENIC BEAUTY

With majestic mountain ranges, enchanting forests, tranquil coastlines, and scenic river valleys, Germany offers a medley of nature at its finest. The country's most prominent geographic feature is the Alps. The snowcapped peaks and deep valleys of this mighty European mountain range offer a host of spectacular sights and a playground for summer and winter sports.

Stretching into Switzerland, Italy, France, Austria, Slovenia, Croatia, Bosnia and Herzegovina, Montenegro, Serbia, and Albania, the Alps run for 750 miles (1,200 km) and cover more than 80,000 square miles (207,000 sq km).[1] The northern section of the Alpine range, the Bavarian Alps, begins in southern Germany. The Zugspitze is the highest Alpine mountain point in Germany at 9,718 feet (2,962 m), and it lies on the border of Germany and Austria.[2] On a clear day, the view from atop this

The Bavarian Alps add picturesque beauty to Germany's landscape.

lofty point extends into four countries: Switzerland, Austria, Italy, and Germany.

> Germany has 1,484 miles (2,389 km) of coastline.

A COUNTRY WITH MANY NEIGHBORS

Germany lies in central Europe and is bordered by Denmark to the north; the Netherlands, Belgium, Luxembourg, and France to the west; Switzerland and Austria to the south; and the Czech Republic and Poland to the east. Germany has shorelines on both the North Sea and the Baltic Sea to the north.

As Europe's seventh-largest country by area, Germany has a territory of 137,847 square miles (357,021 sq km).[3] It is roughly the same size as the state of Montana. Germany is divided into 16 *Länder*, or states, three of which are cities (Berlin, Hamburg, and Bremen). Bavaria, or Bayern in German, is the largest *Länd*, or state.

To the north, Germany meets Denmark on the Jutland Peninsula, where the border is a short 42 miles (68 km).[4] The shores of the peninsula comprise Germany's two stretches of coastline. In the North Sea are the Frisian Islands. Germany controls the East Frisian Islands, while other countries control the West and North Frisian Islands. Across the peninsula, in the Baltic Sea, are the German islands of Rügen, Hiddensee, and Fehmarn. Whereas the Frisian Islands are at a low elevation, the German islands in the Baltic are higher and are rocky with chalky cliffs.

LANDSCAPE

Spreading down from the north, the North Central Plain covers one-third of the country and is nearly flat. This low-lying area consists of mudflats near the coastline but transitions into marshes and wetlands further inland and finally becomes a fertile agricultural area. Heathlands near the coast consist of sand and gravel. As the heathlands are not suitable for growing crops, trees have been planted there instead. Rivers wind through the area on their way to the Baltic and the North Seas. Much of the North Central Plain lies less than 300 feet (91 m) above sea level, and the elevation never exceeds 656 feet (200 m).[5]

To the south of the North Central Plain lies the Central German Uplands. Flat plains and rolling hills spread across this region. A fertile,

THE RHINE RIVER

The Ruhr, Main, and Mosel Rivers are all tributaries of the majestic Rhine River, Germany's most scenic and busiest waterway. The Rhine makes its way through Germany from the Alps in Switzerland and cuts through the Netherlands before emptying into the North Sea. In the southwestern tip of Germany, the Rhine serves as the border with France. The Rhine was long believed to have a length of 820 miles (1,320 km), but in 2010, new calculations determined a shorter distance of approximately 765 miles (1,230 km). The banks of the Rhine are home to numerous vineyards, castles, and fortresses.[6]

Geography of Germany

broad valley called the Thuringian Basin provides rich soil for grain crops, orchards, and vineyards. Near the basin lie the Thuringian Forest and the Harz Mountains. Brocken, the highest point in the Harz Mountains, reaches 3,747 feet (1,142 m).[7] Elsewhere, the elevation in the Central German Uplands is generally between 1,000 and 2,500 feet (300 and 760 m) above sea level.[8] Through the region run the breathtakingly beautiful valleys of the Rhine and the Mosel Rivers. Deep indentations cut rugged gorges through the land through which the Rhine River flows, making it a popular tourist attraction.

Further south lie the South German Hills. This area divides the Central Uplands from the Alps and consists of a series of escarpments, or long, parallel ridges. The lowlands between the ridges boast fertile clay soil, giving the area some of the best farmland in the country. Farmers grow hops and grains used in the production of beer. This region ranges in

LORELEI ROCK

The Lorelei Rock stands at the narrowest point of the Rhine River, on the eastern bank near Koblenz. This mighty rock, which rises nearly 430 feet (131 m) above the water, is said to be home to a beautiful mermaid named Lorelei.[9] According to the myth, Lorelei enchants sailors and fishermen with her beautiful singing and lures them to their deaths in the whirlpools that swirl around her rock. The rock has been the site of many boat accidents, and the mythological mermaid has been the subject of many works of art, including songs, poems, novels, paintings, and operas.

elevation from approximately 500 to 2,500 feet (150 to 762 m).[10] The Rhine, Main, and Danube Rivers all flow through the South German Hills.

Most of Germany's important cities, including Berlin, Munich, Mannheim, Cologne, Bremen, and Hamburg, are located on rivers. Rivers play a vital role in the nation's commercial shipping, especially for the industrial cities located along them. Hamburg, located on the Elbe, is Germany's second-largest city and one of Europe's largest ports. Ships and barges carry goods to the North Sea via the Elbe River.

In the southwestern corner of Germany is located the Schwarzwald, or Black Forest. This mountainous region earns its name from the thick, dark spruce trees that grow

GERMAN LAKES

Germany has few lakes, and the few that exist are concentrated in two areas rather than spread out across the country. Germany's largest lake is Bodensee, or Lake Constance. Located on the nation's southern border and thus shared with Switzerland and Austria, Lake Constance is approximately 40 miles (65 km) long and up to 8 miles (13 km) wide in some spots. It has a surface area of 209 square miles (541 sq km).[11]

Germany's northeast region has a concentration of shallow lakes, the largest of which is Lake Müritz. Second in size to Lake Constance, Lake Müritz lies within Müritz National Park in the Mecklenburg Lake District of Germany.

Cities and villages line the banks of the Rhine River.

there. The Black Forest region is comprised of granite and sandstone uplands with deep, narrow valleys. Although some peaks in the Black Forest reach more than 4,000 feet (1,200 m), the average elevation in the area is between 2,500 and 3,000 feet (762 and 910 m).[12]

The Bavarian Alps, part of Europe's largest mountain system, are found in the south of Germany. Mountain streams flow down the Alps and drain into the Danube River. The area thrives on tourism and offers recreational activities such as skiing, mountain climbing, and hiking. At the foot of the Zugspitze lies the village of Garmisch-Partenkirchen, a world-famous downhill ski area that was home to the 1936 Olympic Winter Games.

CLIMATE

Most of Germany's climate is moderate. The exceptions are the marine climate to the north, on the Baltic and North Seas, and the mountain climate of the Alps, where snow remains on some peaks year-round.

The climate of northwestern Germany is moderated by the North Atlantic Current, a warm ocean current that flows into the North Sea. In this region, winters are gentle and summers are cool, similar to the climate of the northwestern United States. In Germany's southern and eastern regions, a continental climate produces hot summers and cold

Forests and lakes dot the region near the Bavarian Alps.

AVERAGE TEMPERATURES AND RAINFALL

Region (City)	Average January Temperature Minimum/Maximum	Average July Temperature Minimum/Maximum	Average Rainfall January/July
Baltic Coast (Kiel)	28/36°F (−2/2°C)	55/70°F (13/21°C)	2.5/3.0 inches (6.3/7.5 cm)
North Central Plain (Berlin)	27/36°F (−3/2°C)	57/75°F (14/24°C)	1.8/2.9 inches (4.6/7.3 cm)
Central German Uplands (Kassel)	23/34°F (−5/1°C)	55/73°F (13/23°C)	2.3/5.5 inches (5.9/13.9 cm)
Northeast Coastlands (Hamburg)	28/36°F (−2/2°C)	55/72°F (13/22°C)	2.3/3.3 inches (5.8/8.3 cm)
North Rhineland (Frankfurt)	28/37°F (−2/3°C)	59/77°F (15/25°C)	2.3/2.8 inches (5.8/7.0 cm)
Bavarian Alps (Garmisch-Partenkirchen)	19/34°F (−7/1°C)	55/77°F (13/25°C)	2.1/5.3 inches (5.4/13.4 cm)[13]

winters. The northeast region is affected by forceful winds from Russia, which can make winters bitterly cold. Quick variations in the country's climate are possible when moderate westerly winds coming off the Atlantic Ocean collide with cold air masses from northeastern Europe.

The climate of Upper Bavaria is sometimes affected by warm, dry winds passing over the northern portion of the Alps into the Bavarian Plateau. These winds—known as foehns—bring warm weather and clear skies.

Climate of Germany

CHAPTER 3

ANIMALS AND NATURE: CREATURES OF THE FOREST

Germany's national animal is the black eagle, which is said to represent strength and freedom. The black eagle is not an actual species; rather, it is an emblem of heraldry, the system of symbols used in noble families' coats of arms. The bird is depicted on the German coat of arms.

WILDLIFE

With areas of thick forests, rolling hills, wide fields, and rivers, lakes, and mountains, Germany is home to many woodland creatures, including deer, fox, badger, hare, quail, pheasant, lynx, and wild boar. In the Alpine regions of the country, ibex and chamois—both members of

Lynx live in German forests.

One venomous snake can be found in Germany: the adder.

the goat and sheep families—can be found. Otters, badgers, beavers, marten, polecats, European wildcats, and lynx are prevalent in the central to southern regions of the country. Squirrels have become a rare sight in Germany, but hedgehogs live in the countryside.

Although bears and wolves were once plentiful in Germany, both species were hunted to the point of extinction in the nineteenth century. The wolf has been reemerging slowly, with an estimated 50 now living within German borders, but no bears are found in the country.[1] Today, strict hunting regulations throughout Germany protect animals that have dwindling numbers. At the same time, regulations encourage the hunting of animals that overpopulate the country. Following World War II, the wild boar population increased at

GERMAN DOG BREEDS

Many common dog breeds originated in Germany. German shepherds and Rottweilers have long been used as herders, guard dogs, police dogs, and search-and-rescue animals. Dachshunds, with their distinctive short legs and long bodies, were bred to hunt badgers and rabbits. The Weimaraner has a light-gray coat and piercing eyes and was originally used by German royalty to hunt large game. Other popular dog breeds that have come from Germany include the poodle, schnauzer, Doberman pinscher, Pomeranian, German shorthaired pointer, and American Eskimo.

Hedgehogs live in burrows or among the vegetation.

THE WILD BOAR

The wild boar thrives throughout Germany's forest regions. This large mammal is related to the modern pig but is a faster runner and a good swimmer. The boar is covered in dark, coarse, bristly hair and has a long snout and four sharp tusks. It stands approximately 3 feet (91 cm) tall at the shoulders and can grow up to 6 feet (1.8 m) long. Males can weigh in excess of 400 pounds (180 kg), while females are smaller.

Germans hunt wild boars to eat. However, since the Chernobyl nuclear power disaster in the Soviet Union in 1986, the German government has had difficulty dealing with the increasing number of wild boars found to be radioactive. Mushrooms and truffles—favorite foods of the foraging wild boar—absorb high amounts of radiation. Even 25-plus years after the disaster, the vegetation still contains radiation, which poisons the boars that eat it. Wild boars killed in Germany are tested for radiation, and the German government pays hunters for any boars that are inedible due to radiation poisoning.

an alarming rate. Legalized hunting brought down the number of those potentially dangerous tusked boars, lowering the threat to people and crops.

BIRDS, WATERFOWL, AND FISH

Ducks, geese, and swans are plentiful in Germany, due, in part, to the country's several internationally recognized bird reserves. The 74,767-acre (30,257-ha) Schaalsee, or "Lake Schaal," Biosphere Reserve provides a habitat for sea eagles, graylag geese, cranes, osprey, and other birds.[2] The nation's lakes also play a

Germany is working to protect white storks.

vital role in the European migration of ducks, geese, and other waterfowl.

Although rare, the white-tailed eagle can be found near the lakes of the North Central Plain. The golden eagle makes its home in the Alps. The white stork, which continues to drop in number, can occasionally be found perched atop chimneys. This bird is naturally attracted to unpolluted, undrained marshlands but now has difficulty finding such areas. Efforts are underway to designate reserve areas for this bird and rebuild its population.

Germany's waters contain a variety of fish, from salmon and trout in Alpine mountain springs to the deep-sea cod of the Baltic Sea. Fishermen catch cod, herring, mackerel, shrimp, carp, pike, and perch from the country's oceans, rivers, and lakes.

FLORA

Nearly 30 percent of Germany is covered by forests.[3] The Black Forest in the southwest is known for evergreen trees so dark they appear black. In the east, the Bavarian Forest meets the Czech Bohemian Forest at the border, forming the largest forest in Europe.

Northern pike swim in German lakes.

The woodlands of the North Central Plain were once predominantly oak and other hardwoods. However, these trees were cut down hundreds of years ago, and heather was planted in their place for sheep grazing. Altering the landscape in this way resulted in soil erosion, and in time very few trees of any value could grow in the sandy soil left behind. In the nineteenth century, fertilizer was used to improve the soil for future agriculture, and softwoods—mostly Scotch pine trees—were planted in an effort at reforestation.

Beech trees flourish in the Central German Uplands, and in the mountainous regions, spruce and fir trees grow. Balsam, willow herb, foxglove, and monkshood are common throughout the country. Forest floors with good soil and ample light produce dog's mercury, sweet woodruff, and violets. In springtime, wildflowers burst to life, dotting the mountain slopes with color. In northern Germany, fields of purple heather and yellow rapeseed blanket the countryside.

ENVIRONMENTAL THREATS

Germany's rapid reconstruction after World War II caused harmful emissions from coal-burning utilities to be released into the air and then fall back to Earth as acid rain. In 1980, acid rain was first detected when trees began dying. Since that time, Germany has worked hard to pass strict regulations that limit pollution caused by automobiles and industry.

Wildflowers such as heather bloom across Germany in the spring.

ENDANGERED SPECIES IN GERMANY

According to the International Union for Conservation of Nature (IUCN), Germany is home to the following numbers of species that are categorized by the organization as Critically Endangered, Endangered, or Vulnerable:

Mammals	6
Birds	6
Reptiles	0
Amphibians	0
Fishes	21
Mollusks	10
Other Invertebrates	24
Plants	12
Total	79[4]

Antipollution laws call for hefty fines on industries that discharge poisonous emissions.

In 1986, a fire at a chemical plant along the Rhine River on the border between Germany and Switzerland caused more than 30 short tons (27 metric tons) of poisonous agricultural chemicals to be washed into the waterway. With that single event, more than ten years of river cleanup efforts were undone. Within ten days, the pollutants had traveled the length of the river and into the North Sea, killing hundreds of thousands of fish and wiping out some species entirely. The accident was a terrible blow to Germany's ecological health.

Demonstrators held a requiem for the Rhine in response to the 1986 chemical fire.

Facing public outcry, the government organized the Rhine Action Programme of 1987. The successful program cut pollution dramatically and cleaned up the river so fish could again thrive. A new environmental project, the Rhine 2020 Programme, is currently underway, and its goal is to make the river clean enough for swimmers.

Germany has also worked hard to protect its forests. In 1999, the country joined a United Nations initiative aimed at addressing the problems of deforestation. Germany was so successful with its regional

Thanks to the country's conservation efforts, Germany's forests, including Berchtesgaden National Park, are growing.

and national programs that the forests there have actually expanded instead of decreasing in size.

Although Germany was slow to recognize environmental concerns, it has made remarkable strides in cleaning up and focusing on a healthy environment. Today, Germany is one of the world's "greenest" countries, building up renewable energy sources, clamping down on emissions, investing in green technology, and putting the pressure on other countries to do the same. The country has made a remarkable recovery following the environmental devastation that occurred just decades ago.

NATIONAL PARKS

In 1970, the Bavarian Forest National Park became Germany's first national park. Today, there are 14 national parks and more than 100 nature parks within the country, all of which have a special focus on preserving natural beauty, conserving natural resources, and maintaining biodiversity.[5] Germany's national parks include the following:

- Bavarian Forest National Park
- Berchtesgaden National Park
- Eifel National Park
- Hainich National Park
- Hamburg Wadden Sea National Park
- Harz National Park
- Jasmund National Park
- Kellerwald-Edersee National Park
- Lower Oder Valley National Park
- Lower Saxony Wadden Sea National Park
- Müritz National Park
- Saxon Switzerland National Park
- Schleswig-Holstein Wadden Sea National Park
- West-Pomeranian Boddenlandschaft National Park

CHAPTER 4

HISTORY:
AN IMPERIAL PAST

The first of the ancient Germanic peoples were small migrant tribes of warriors. These people migrated from eastern Eurasia and northern Europe, roaming the lands to hunt and farm. They settled in small groups in what is now northern Germany and southern Scandinavia during the Northern European Bronze Age, approximately 1700 to 450 BCE. Two principal cultures were the Celts and the Germans.

ROMANS, GERMANS, FRANKS

Starting in approximately the second century BCE, the powerful Roman Empire began expanding northward. The Germanic peoples fought several battles against the invading Romans, winning some and losing others. Finally, a German confederation led by Hermann, or Arminius in Latin, defeated three legions of Roman soldiers in the Battle of the Teutoburg

Celtic sword hilts dating from the twelfth to eighth centuries BCE

THE ROMAN VIEWPOINT

Roman historian Tacitus wrote *The Germania* in 98 CE, identifying many Germanic tribes. He described the Germans as large, brave soldiers and capable women who were moral and chaste. The Germans, he added, placed great importance on their successes in battle. Tacitus also claimed (although it was not strictly true) that the Germans were a pure-blooded race, free from evidence of intermixture with foreigners. He wrote:

> "Hence amongst such a mighty multitude of men, the same make and form is found in all, eyes stern and blue, yellow hair. . . . In the number of their herds they rejoice; and these are their . . . most desirable riches. . . . Swords they rarely use, or the larger spear. They carry javelins or, in their own language, *framms*, pointed with a piece of iron short and narrow, but so sharp and manageable, that with the same weapon they can fight at a distance or hand to hand, just as need requires."[1]

Forest in 9 CE. Following this defeat, Roman Emperor Augustus Caesar halted his attempts to conquer the Germanic tribes east of the Rhine River. The Romans then built a long wall between the Rhine and Danube Rivers to protect Roman territory from attacks.

By the fifth century, Germanic tribes such as the Goths, Vandals, and Burgundians had spread throughout the regions of present-day Italy, Britain, France, Spain, and Germany. Germanic troops moved into Rome, contributing to the fall of the Roman Empire in 476 CE.

Germanic tribes sacked Rome in 410 CE.

Following the fall of Rome, the Franks became powerful in present-day France, Belgium, and western Germany, and by the eighth century they had conquered all the Germanic tribes except the Saxons. The Frankish king Charlemagne (742–814) became ruler over much of western Europe, from northeastern Spain and Italy to Denmark. His empire became known as the Holy Roman Empire. Charlemagne died in 814, but his grandsons broke the kingdom into three parts in 843 and ruled until 911.

The Hohenstaufen dynasty ruled Germany and the Holy Roman Empire for much of the twelfth and thirteenth centuries with only brief interruptions. In 1273, the German princes elected a new emperor who took the name Rudolf I of Hapsburg. Members of three different royal families reigned until 1438, when

REFORMATION AND THE THIRTY YEARS' WAR

Until the sixteenth century, the Catholic Church in Rome and the ruling powers of the Holy Roman Empire were intertwined. As the Hapsburgs grew in power, so did the wealth and power of the church. But in 1517, a German monk and professor named Martin Luther challenged the power of the Catholic Church. His criticism of the church led to the Protestant Reformation. Protestantism spread throughout Germany and then the rest of Europe.

The Catholic Church began a Counter-Reformation. Between 1618 and 1648, the Thirty Years' War was fought to reverse the spread of Protestantism. Finally, in 1648, the Treaty of Westphalia was signed, which specified that the religion of the king would be the religion of the people.

the crown returned to the Hapsburgs, who ruled the Holy Roman Empire until 1806.

THE RISE OF PRUSSIA

In the mid-seventeenth century, Frederick William of Brandenburg took control over Prussia, an area in northeastern Germany. By 1701, Brandenburg-Prussia had become an independent kingdom, which would later be called simply Prussia. Over the years, Prussia grew in size, as did Austria, until in the late eighteenth century the two had become the most powerful kingdoms in German-speaking central Europe.

In 1862, Otto von Bismarck (1815–1898) was appointed minister-president of Prussia by King William I. Bismarck helped Prussia expand its power and territory and unify the German states through three wars against Denmark, Austria, and France. As a result of the national enthusiasm that Bismarck cultivated, many Germans desired a single German nation instead of a confederation of member-states. After Bismarck's success in the Franco-Prussian War of 1870–1871, the German Empire, or *Reich*, was formed. The remaining four southern German states joined the federation. On January 18, 1871, Wilhelm I was crowned the first kaiser, or emperor, of the new German Empire. He appointed Bismarck as chancellor and head of government.

A previous revolution in 1848 failed to unite the German principalities.

In 1890, Wilhelm II, grandson of Wilhelm I, forced Bismarck to resign, then began increasing the country's military and naval might. As a result of rapid industrialization, Germany became the most powerful country in continental Europe.

Germany's neighbors grew concerned over Wilhelm's aggressive pursuits. In 1907, the United Kingdom, France, and Russia, which had been colonial rivals, formed an alliance called the Triple Entente. In opposition, Germany, Austria-Hungary, and a somewhat reluctant Italy came together as the Triple Alliance. With the formation of these alliances, Europe was divided into two increasingly hostile blocs.

WORLD WAR I

On June 28, 1914, Archduke Franz Ferdinand (1863–1914) of Austria-Hungary and his wife were shot and killed in Sarajevo, a city in Austrian-ruled Bosnia-Herzegovina, by an assassin hired by the Serbian secret service. Spurred on by Germany, Austria-Hungary officially declared war against Serbia one month later. This event triggered World War I as the other European countries joined the hostilities to defend their allies. Germany, Austria-Hungary, and their smaller allies became known as the Central powers, while the nations opposing them became the Allied powers.

Wilhelm I died in 1888; his son Frederick III reigned for 99 days and then the throne passed to Wilhelm II.

World War I (1914–1918) dragged on for four years, with millions of soldiers on each side dying in the trenches.

Otto von Bismarck

German troops fighting in trenches
in World War I

The stalemate was broken when the United States joined the war on the Allied side. On November 11, 1918, Germany surrendered. The end of the war was technically known as an armistice, or a temporary cease-fire, but in fact the German armies had been decisively defeated. On June 28, 1919, the Treaty of Versailles was signed. It did not assign formal blame for starting the war, but Germany had to accept responsibility for the damage it had caused.

Approximately 1.7 million Germans were killed during World War I.[2] Following the war, Germany lost its overseas colonies to various Allied powers, as well as certain border areas to France, Poland, Belgium, and Denmark. In addition, the country was disarmed and limited to an army of only 100,000 men.[3] The victorious Allied powers also tried to impose billions of dollars of reparations on Germany, but the Germans did not accept the outcome of the war and refused to pay most of the penalty.

THE WEIMAR REPUBLIC AND THE RISE OF HITLER

In the hope of obtaining better terms in the Treaty of Versailles, Germany declared itself a republic. A new constitution was drawn up for what was soon called the Weimar Republic. But the new government faced numerous challenges. To pay subsidies to its citizens and evade the payment of reparations, the German government simply began printing more money. This action started a cycle of high inflation. By November 1923, the old German currency was worthless.

An international committee headed by Americans reestablished German currency and finance, and, with support from generous US loans, five years of prosperity resulted. After the Great Depression began in 1929, however, Germany soon had millions of unemployed citizens desperate for work and money. Members of the middle classes who had lost their savings in the great inflation and workers who had lost their jobs in the Depression were eager for a political leader who would pull them out of despair.

The Nationalist Socialist German Workers' Party, or Nazis, seemed to many Germans to offer the solution. The Nazi leader, Adolf Hitler, maneuvered skillfully until Germany's aging president appointed him chancellor on January 30, 1933. After the president died in 1934, Hitler combined the positions of chancellor and president and became the führer, or absolute leader. The Nazis called the new regime the Third Reich, or the Third Empire, after the Holy Roman Empire and Kaiser Wilhelm's second empire.

Although rearmament had secretly begun under the Weimar Republic, Hitler openly disobeyed the peace treaty and began building a massive army. He was a powerful, rousing speaker, able to rally Germans around his cause. He also drew support by reducing unemployment, creating jobs in road construction, public works projects, and, ultimately, weapons manufacturing. Unfortunately, Hitler's vision of a revived Germany would ultimately take the country down a deadly and destructive path.

Kids used blocks of worthless German money to play in 1923.

The German people hoped Adolf Hitler would improve their lives.

NAZI GERMANY AND WORLD WAR II

Hitler and his Nazi followers blamed the Jews, Communists, Slavs, and other minority groups for the state of affairs in Germany. The Nazis used the term *Aryan*—the name of an ancient tribe of Germanic people—to describe people they believed to be of pure Germanic heritage. These people were supposed to be blond with blue eyes, although Hitler himself had dark hair. The Nazis' plan for racial supremacy included purifying the Aryan race by destroying the Jews and extending Aryan rule over the supposedly inferior Slavic peoples to the east. The huge Propaganda Ministry, run by Joseph Goebbels, took over the press, the movies, and the mass media and carried on a campaign of hatred against non-Aryans. Dissenters landed in concentration camps. Hitler stripped the Jews of their civil rights and monetary assets, causing several hundred thousand of them to flee for their lives.[4]

Hitler wanted to make Germany the most powerful country in Europe once again and eventually in the world. He began

THE NIGHT OF BROKEN GLASS

On the night of November 9, 1938, and into the next morning, Propaganda Minister Joseph Goebbels arranged for members of Nazi youth groups and the special police to smash windows of Jewish shops and to burn synagogues throughout Nazi-controlled territory. The ensuing devastation was known as *Kristallnacht*, "Crystal Night," or the Night of Broken Glass. Following Kristallnacht, those Jews who had remained in the country knew they would be in danger if they stayed. Those who could find refuge abroad began to flee, even though they had to give up their property and start their lives over.

working toward that goal in March 1938 by taking over Austria. He took over the Sudetenland from Czechoslovakia in October 1938 and invaded Czechoslovakia in March 1939. He invaded Poland on September 1 of that year. Recognizing too late that Hitler could not be reasoned with, the United Kingdom and France declared war on Germany on September 3, 1939, marking the official beginning of World War II.

In the spring of 1940, Hitler's troops captured Denmark, Norway, the Netherlands, Belgium, Luxembourg, and France. The German army, called the Wehrmacht, won quick victories by employing a new form of war called blitzkrieg, or "lightning war," which involved the coordinated use of masses of tanks protected by aircraft. After defeating France, Hitler began bombing the United Kingdom, preparing to invade that country. Under the leadership of Prime Minister Winston Churchill, however, the British successfully resisted.

For the first two years of the war, it seemed that nothing could stop Germany and its allies, Italy and Japan, which comprised the Axis powers. The tide began to turn, however, for two reasons. First of all, Hitler underestimated the difficulty of conquering the Soviet Union after launching a massive invasion in June 1941. And second, in December, the Allied powers were joined by the United States, with its tremendous industrial might, after Japan bombed the US naval base at Pearl Harbor.

Thousands of Nazi troops line up for Hitler's inspection in Nuremberg, Germany, in 1938.

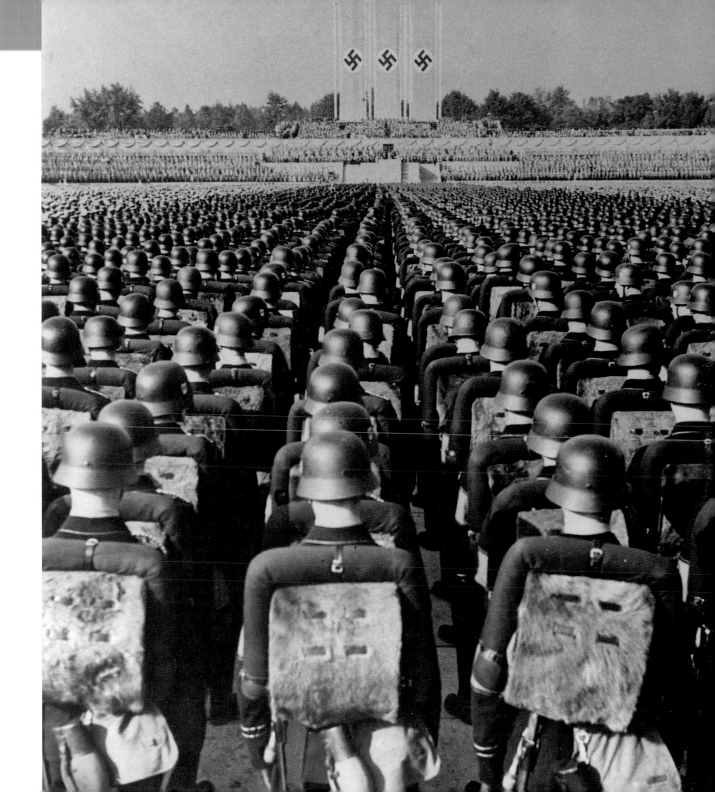

GERMANY'S DARKEST HOUR:
THE HOLOCAUST

Hitler viewed his early victories as evidence that the Germans were truly a superior race. The Nazis focused not simply on conquering territories but on reorganizing Europe along racial lines. Earlier, they had sent so-called domestic enemies—including Communists, homosexuals, and Roma (also known as gypsies)—to concentration camps, and they had killed people in institutions with mental and physical disabilities. After the 1941 invasion of the Soviet Union, the Nazis instigated what they called the Final Solution against the Jews. Jews from all over Europe were rounded up and sent to concentration camps, where most were either killed on arrival or worked to death. In what is now called the Holocaust, Nazi troops murdered 6 million Jews and millions of other non-Aryan civilians and enslaved several million more, who were forced to work under terrible conditions to serve the German war effort.[5]

> The word *Holocaust* comes from a Greek word meaning "sacrifice by fire."

By the end of 1944, troops from the Soviet Union and the western Allied nations had descended on Germany. Although most Germans remained faithful to their führer to the end, Hitler realized he had lost the war and committed suicide on April 30, 1945. Germany surrendered eight days later, on May 7.

Children imprisoned at the Auschwitz concentration camp

GERMANY FOLLOWING WORLD WAR II

At the end of World War II, Germany lay in ruin. Its cities had been reduced to rubble by US and British bombing. The Allied powers divided Germany into four zones, each to be occupied by one of the Allies: the United States, the United Kingdom, France, and the Soviet Union. The first three countries took steps to create democratic governments in their zones, but the Soviet Union established a Communist-controlled police state in its zone, East Germany. Each of the four countries governed a segment of Germany's capital city, Berlin. In 1948, the western Allies introduced a new currency to promote economic revival. The Soviet Union retaliated by cutting off access to Berlin, which lay in the middle of its zone. What became known as the Cold War developed between the now-divided Allies.

In 1949, Germany split into two countries. The three western zones of Germany were united to form the Federal Republic of Germany (FRG), otherwise known as West Germany. A democratic government was established, and citizens elected their leaders. The remaining zone, occupied by the Soviets, became the German Democratic Republic (GDR), or East Germany. In this Communist-led country, industry and large holdings of land were taken under government control and nationalized.

Although Berlin lay wholly in East Germany, more than 100 miles (161 km) from the border with West Germany, the city was also split in two. East Berlin belonged to East Germany, and West Berlin belonged to West Germany.

Economic growth in the two countries diverged. The United States helped West Germany recover rapidly. Meanwhile, the Soviet Union drained East Germany of industrial resources to rebuild its own infrastructure. As the East German economy began to suffer, East Germans began leaving the country. Their easiest route was to go from East Berlin to West Berlin. To stem the loss of population, East Germany erected a 28-mile (45-km) wall in 1961, dividing East Berlin from West Berlin with bricks and barbed wire.[6] Checkpoints ringed

THE BERLIN AIRLIFT

When the Allies economically united their three zones in Berlin and introduced a shared currency, the move angered the Soviets, who believed the Allies were violating the treaty. As a result, the Soviets declared the Allies had no authority in Berlin. The Soviets set up a blockade, cutting off all highway, railway, and water traffic through the Soviet-controlled portion of East Germany into Berlin. West Berliners found themselves completely cut off from all supplies.

In a massive effort to assist the people of West Berlin, US and British planes began dropping food, coal, petroleum, machinery, and other necessary supplies into the city. What became known as the Berlin airlift began in late June 1948 and lasted until September 1949. In all, US and British pilots flew more than 250,000 missions.[7] They dropped 2.3 million short tons (2.09 million metric tons) of food and supplies.[8]

the entire city of West Berlin, making it difficult for unauthorized people to cross the border.

With the Berlin Wall in place, it became very hard for anyone to leave East Berlin—or East Germany in general. Citizens needed special permission to cross into West Berlin. Many East Germans tried to escape into the West. At least 136 people died at the Berlin Wall, as well as at least 251 others at various border checkpoints.[9]

A COUNTRY REUNITED

For nearly 30 years, the Berlin Wall divided the city. But in the late 1980s, Mikhail Gorbachev, president of the Soviet Union, initiated a new set of freedoms for the Soviets, which included some freedom of speech and a general opening up of the government. In 1989, people in Communist Eastern European countries began protesting and demanding that repressive leaders be removed from office. On October 18, the East Germans were successful in removing Communist leader Erich Honecker from power.

Less than one month later, on November 9, 1989, the Berlin Wall was opened, and rejoicing Germans physically tore it down. The following year, on October 3, 1990, East Germany and West Germany reunited as one nation, the Federal Republic of Germany. West German chancellor Helmut Kohl became the chancellor of the unified Germany and was reelected in December 1990 in the country's first all-German election. On March 15, 1991, the countries that had once occupied Germany following World War II gave up territorial rights and control.

Following reunification, much work was needed to modernize the former East Germany. West Germans worried that East Germans would pour into their towns and cities and take jobs at much lower wages. Leaders of the new Federal Republic of Germany worked hard to ensure that wages, benefits, and pensions in the former East Germany were swiftly equalized with those in West Germany so the country might move past its divided history and toward a unified future. Unfortunately, East German industry remained uncompetitive, and 15 years later, the eastern region of the united country still lagged behind in productivity.

CHANCELLOR KOHL

Chancellor Helmut Kohl (1930–) will always be remembered as the leader who reunified East and West Germany. He signed the reunification treaty on October 3, 1990, and remained the country's chancellor until 1998. In November 1990, one month after the country was reunited, Kohl rejoiced at a campaign rally:

"Look back over those 58 years: war, misery, suffering, bombing attacks, brutal rule by the Nazi regime, the division of our city and our country. This is a happy hour! Our unity was won without war, without bloody revolution, without killings or executions. . . . That is the message of Germany today. Let the message of peace go forth from German soil!"[10]

In the 1950s, West Germany had joined other European nations in forming a treaty establishing the European Community. A second treaty, signed at Maastricht in the Netherlands in 1992, provided for the introduction of a new, shared currency, called the euro, to replace the separate currencies of many members of the European Union (EU), the modern organization that had grown out of the European Community. Euro notes and coins went into circulation in Germany on January 1, 2002, phasing out the old and much-beloved currency, the deutsche mark.

Helmut Kohl was the longest-serving German chancellor since Bismarck.

The Berlin Wall, which divided democratic West Germany from Communist East Germany, was opened in 1989.

CHAPTER 5

PEOPLE: NATIONAL PRIDE

In 2011, Germany was home to an estimated 81,471,834 people, making it the sixteenth most populated country in the world and the second most populated country in Europe, after Russia.[1] Germany is densely populated, with 591 people per square mile (228 per sq km).[2] In contrast, neighboring France has approximately 295 people per square mile (114 per sq km).[3] The United States has only 83 people per square mile (32 per sq km).[4] But not all of the people living in Germany are permanent German residents.

WHO LIVES IN GERMANY?

Native Germans make up approximately 91.5 percent of the country's population.[5] These people claim to descend from a long history of

During festivals and holidays, some Germans dress in traditional Bavarian clothing.

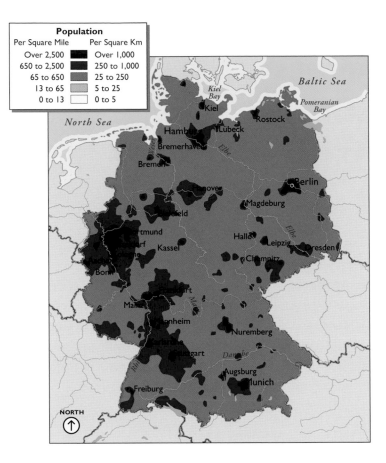

Population Density of Germany

Germanic peoples, including the tribes of the Franks, Saxons, Bavarians, and Swabians. Of course, with few natural borders such as rivers, Germany has become home to many immigrants over the years. Today, minority groups, comprising approximately 7 million people, include a large number of immigrants from Turkey, as well as people from Italy, Greece, Poland, Russia, Serbia, and Croatia.[6] Most immigrants come to Germany looking for work, although some come seeking refuge from political conflict in their homelands.

German laws have made it difficult for foreigners to become German citizens unless they can trace their ancestry to Germany. These laws are slowly changing, however. The country has also struggled with attacks on foreigners by neo-Nazi groups, or skinheads, although such groups remain small. Germany continues to deal with the delicate issue of national pride and balancing the concerns of a multicultural population.

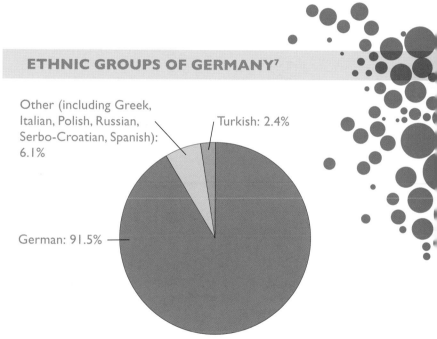

ETHNIC GROUPS OF GERMANY[7]

Other (including Greek, Italian, Polish, Russian, Serbo-Croatian, Spanish): 6.1%

Turkish: 2.4%

German: 91.5%

GUEST WORKERS

In the 1960s and 1970s, an influx of *Gastarbeiter*, or "guest workers," poured into the country to take blue-collar jobs that Germans were not eager to have. Most of these unskilled laborers came from Turkey, although the first waves of Gastarbeiter were from Italy and the former Yugoslavia. Germany's program for guest workers allowed them to remain in the country for only one to two years, after which they had to return to their homelands. However, many workers did not return but had their families join them in Germany instead. Thus, Germany has a large and rapidly increasing number of Turkish people. Nearly 2 million Turks live in Germany, comprising the largest group of foreigners in the country.[9] Germany has the largest population of Turks outside Turkey.[10]

When the Berlin Wall came down in 1989 and East and West Germany were reunified, millions of former East Germans eventually lost their jobs. German frustration grew against the Gastarbeiter who still lingered in the country or brought their families to join them. Many Germans felt available jobs should go to native Germans instead of immigrants, and many were angered by the financial strain that this influx of people placed on the nation's schools and welfare program. Resentment grew toward Turks and other minorities living in Germany. The country continues to deal with this conflict.

DEMOGRAPHICS

Nearly two-thirds of all German citizens are between the ages of 15 and 64. Approximately 20 percent of the population is 65 years or older, and 13.3 percent is 14 years or younger. In 2011, the life expectancy was 77.82 years for German men and 82.44 years for German women. At an average of 80.07 years, Germany has a life expectancy among the top 30 countries in the world.[8]

The birth rate in Germany has declined over the years. In 2011, the country's birth rate was 8.3 births per 1,000 citizens. Currently, Germany has negative population growth, meaning that there are more deaths than births.

On average, women give birth to 1.41 children.[11] Therefore, the majority of mothers (particularly those of native origin) have only one child. To combat long-term population decline, the government provides incentives, including tax cuts, for families and child care subsidies.

Approximately 74 percent of the total population in Germany resides in urban areas, including cities and towns. The remainder lives in rural areas, including small villages. Added together, Germany's four largest cities—Berlin, Hamburg, Munich, and Cologne—are home to approximately 7.5 million people.[12]

Most Germans live in urban areas.

THE GERMAN LANGUAGE

The borders of today's Germany are relatively new, and the idea of Germany as a unified country is less than two centuries old. Thus, Germany is not the only country where German is spoken. Austria and Liechtenstein are German-speaking countries, and large numbers of people in Luxembourg, Switzerland, and parts of northern Italy speak German as well.

YOU SAY IT!

English	Standard German
Yes/No	Ja/Nein (yah/nine)
Please	Bitte (BIHT-uh)
Thank you	Danke (DAHN-kuh)
Good day	Guten Tag (GOO-tehn tahk)
Good-bye	Auf Wiedersehen (owf VEE-dur-zayn)

Many dialects of the German language are spoken in different regions of the country. But two main forms of German are spoken: High German in the center and southern portion of the country and Low German in the north. High German is also known as Standard German, as it is the form used for public communication, in schools, and on television.

RELIGION

The Basic Law, Germany's constitution, allows for freedom of religion for all citizens. Most Germans are Christian. Approximately 34 percent are Roman Catholic, and another 34 percent are Protestant, most of whom are Lutheran. There are also small groups of Baptists, Calvinists, Pentecostals, and other Christian denominations. Muslims total 3.4 percent of the

UNIQUE SOUNDS AND LETTERS

The German language uses a punctuation mark called an umlaut, which is written as two dots above a vowel. The umlaut changes the pronunciation of the vowel, raising it in pitch, which usually forces the speaker to pucker his or her lips to produce the sound. When translating a German word with an umlaut into English, the dots are dropped from the vowel and an e is added after it. Thus, *Müller* becomes *Mueller* and *Göring* becomes *Goering*.

Another unique characteristic of German is the use of the letter *ß*, or *Eszett*, as it is called in German. The *ß* is used in place of a double S, as in *grüßen* (GROO-sehn), which means "to greet." In 1996, spelling reform minimized the use of this German letter, although it is still regularly seen throughout Germany. Most commonly, it appears on street signs in the German word for "street," which is *Straße* (SHTRAH-suh).

population.[13] Another large proportion of Germans are atheist or do not participate in religion, especially in the former East Germany.

Today, only a minority of Germans attend church regularly. However, the country does observe Sunday as a day of rest. Under the *Ladenschlussgesetz*, or "shop-closing law," all shops and stores remain closed on Sundays, except for vital businesses such as gas stations and pharmacies.

Before the decimation of the Jewish population during the Holocaust of World War II, approximately 500,000 Jews lived and worked in Germany.[14] After the war, fewer than 25,000 remained in the country. Since World War II, as a result of immigration from Russia, Germany's Jewish population has risen to approximately 120,000.[15]

Berlin is the center of Islam in Germany because of the high concentration of Turks living there. Mosques and Islamic schools have opened in Berlin and Cologne, and Muslim employees are free to carry out daily prayers while at work.

Catholics, Lutherans, Calvinists, and Jews all pay a church tax above their regular income tax. During the 1990s, nearly 4 million Christians left their churches, and some policy makers attribute the change at least in part to the church tax.[16]

The Church of Our Lady in Dresden

CHAPTER 6

CULTURE:
A CLASSICAL
TRADITION

Germany has shared with the world its rich culture, including classical music that has endured for centuries. Orchestras worldwide continue to perform many works of famous German composers.

Johann Sebastian Bach (1685–1750) is considered one of the greatest composers of all time. He wrote more than 1,000 church and instrumental pieces, including such well-known works as Mass in B Minor and the Brandenburg Concertos. One of his most famous and enduring short pieces, "Jesu, Joy of Man's Desiring," is often performed today at weddings.

One of Bach's contemporaries, George Frideric Handel (1685–1759), was greatly influenced by Italian composers and spent much of

The music of many German composers is played throughout the world.

his later life in England. He composed numerous operas and oratorios, the most famous of which is *The Messiah*. Other popular works include the orchestral suites *Water Music* and *Music for the Royal Fireworks,* both marked by their grandeur.

Ludwig van Beethoven (1770–1827) revolutionized classical music. Writing sonatas, symphonies, concertos, and quartets, Beethoven struggled heroically against his gradual loss of hearing, finally becoming totally deaf in 1819. Despite his lack of hearing, Beethoven continued to compose. He wrote some of his most important works—including Symphony no. 9, with its famous chorus "Ode to Joy"—without ever hearing them out loud. The city of Bonn, where Beethoven was born, holds a Beethoven festival every September and October.

Other prominent German composers include Felix Mendelssohn (1809–1847) and Robert Schumann (1810–1856). In addition to Mendelssohn's musical achievements, he was responsible for reviving interest in the works of Bach nearly 80 years after the death of the great composer. Schumann was a leading composer of the German romantic period and is remembered for his beautiful piano compositions.

Richard Wagner (1813–1883) was responsible for changing German opera, combining elements of music, poetry, and theatrical design. He used folktales, myths, and legends to create his operas, the most famous of which are *Lohengrin* and *The Ring of the Nibelung*. Each year, the Bayreuth Festival honors Wagner and his operas.

Beethoven was born in Bonn, Germany, but lived most of his life in Vienna, Austria.

Ludwig van Beethoven composed some of his best work after he went deaf.

Prior to World War II, Germans began exploring more modern tastes in music, including cabaret and swing music. But the Nazis banned these types of music, especially swing, which they viewed as African American in origin. The Nazis also disapproved of jazz because of their racial prejudice, and they feared modern music might fuel a youth rebellion.

Following World War II, popular music in Germany was heavily influenced by US and British bands and singers, and English-language songs became increasingly popular. German pop and rock bands that have attained international success include the rock group Scorpions, which had several chart toppers in the 1980s, and Rammstein, a rock group from East Berlin that became prominent in the 1990s. Young Germans listen to rock, pop, hip-hop, and other forms of popular music from Europe, the United States, and the United Kingdom.

GERMAN MUSIC TODAY

Young Germans listen to a variety of types of music, but rock, hip-hop, and heavy metal are particularly popular. Several groups have emerged as German music superstars, including punk rock group Die Toten Hosen, heavy metal group Rammstein, and teenage band Tokio Hotel. Over the past decade, Silbermond (German for "silver moon"), a rock band from Saxony, has had several chart toppers and received many awards. Alternative pop band Juli (German for "July"), featuring lead singer Eva Briegel, has also made its mark on German music.

The German band Rammstein performs in concert, 2002.

GERMAN LITERATURE

All forms of literature have long flourished in Germany. For hundreds of years, theater has played an important role in German culture, and today, the nation has more than 350 theaters.[1] The arts are of the utmost importance in Germany, and the government subsidizes theaters, operas, and symphonies to ensure that culture thrives and that citizens of average income can afford to attend cultural events.

One of the most influential European writers of all time, Johann Wolfgang von Goethe (1749–1832), was born in Frankfurt. A successful poet, novelist, and playwright, he is perhaps best known for *Faust,* a poetic drama about a man who sells his soul to the devil in exchange for total knowledge. Not only did this drama become a

A PROMISE AND A PLAY

In 1633, the bubonic plague was ravishing the Bavarian village of Oberammergau. The villagers vowed that if God spared them they would perform a play every ten years depicting the Passion of Jesus Christ, which encompassed his life, suffering, and death. After the promise was made, no more villagers succumbed to the plague.

The townspeople of Oberammergau performed the first Passion play the following year, and they have continued to do so every decade since then, except during World War II in 1940. The entire community of approximately 2,000 people comes together to produce the drama; participants must have lived in the village for at least 20 years. Every ten years, thousands of people come from around the world to see the famous Passion play of Oberammergau.

popular work of literature, but it also served as the basis of operas by Charles Gounod and Hector Berlioz.

Bertolt Brecht (1898–1956), Peter Weiss (1916–1982), and Günter Grass (1927–) all penned plays that address social and political issues. Grass, Thomas Mann, Hermann Hesse, and Heinrich Böll are among the many Germans who have won the Nobel Prize in Literature.

The Grimm Brothers, Jacob (1785–1863) and Wilhelm (1786–1859), compiled a collection of native folktales, known as *Grimm's Fairy Tales*. In their effort to preserve these stories, which had previously been passed down orally, the brothers captured popular tales such as "Hansel and Gretel," "Snow White," "Cinderella," and "Little Red Riding Hood."

The original Grimm fairy tales are often darker and more horrific than the modern versions.

GERMAN CINEMA

Between World War I and World War II, German cinema flourished. Throughout the 1920s and 1930s, German filmmakers became renowned for their use of unique camera angles and lighting to create the mood of the film, a style called Expressionism. Fantasy, legend, and psychological realism became the focus of many films of the era, and elements of the supernatural were often used to display the darker fringes of the human experience. Fritz Lang, F. W. Murnau, and G. W. Pabst were some of the leading directors of this time.

Prior to World War II, several influential German moviemakers left the country and fled to the United States, some of them achieving success in US filmmaking. For those who remained in Germany, such as actress and director Leni Riefenstahl, the war brought new filmmaking projects. Propaganda films were made to support the nation's war effort. Riefenstahl's *Triumph of the Will,* an acclaimed yet controversial masterpiece, painted a powerful picture of the Nazi Party during the 1934 Nuremberg Nazi Party Congress.

German filmmaking became stagnant following the war and remained so up until the 1960s. Then, a resurgence in the German film industry began to take place with the Young German Film movement. The 1981 film *Das Boot* still holds the record for the most Academy Award nominations for a German film.

German-born film star Marlene Dietrich rose to international fame and moved to Hollywood in 1930. Contemporary director Wolfgang Petersen has also risen to international status. His works include *Das Boot, The Perfect Storm, The NeverEnding Story, Air Force One,* and *Troy.*

TRADITIONAL, FOLK, AND MODERN ARTS

Artisans and craftspeople in Germany take pride in practicing traditional methods, which often involve hand carving and similarly detailed work. Among the country's best-known products are cuckoo clocks, nutcrackers, violins, porcelain goods, pewter steins, and fine embroidered linens.

In the fifteenth and sixteenth centuries, in order to reproduce an image with a printing press, the image had to be an engraving or a woodcut. Albrecht Dürer (1471–1528) painted, drew, and carved such detailed woodcuts that he is regarded as one of the finest artists in German history.

In more recent times, the German Expressionist movement involved architecture, painting, and cinema. Dark and moody, Expressionist works feature sharp angles, shadows, and geometrically exaggerated elements. As such, Expressionist elements provided the perfect backdrop for the monster movies that became popular in Hollywood during the 1930s, many of

German cuckoo clock

which involved German cinematographers such as Karl Freund. German Expressionism is still evident today in the dark and eerie films of US filmmaker Tim Burton.

Regional music, including the Bavarian oompah bands, can be found throughout Germany. Folk dancers participate in Schuhplattling, a dance that consists of slapping the body and shoes in a fixed pattern. Another common German dance is the polka, danced to the cheerful music of the same name.

CELEBRATING HOLIDAYS AND FESTIVALS

Germans celebrate at least ten official holidays, including New Year's Day, Good Friday, Easter, Pentecost (50 days following Easter), Labor Day (May 1), and Christmas. Other religious holidays include the Feast of Corpus Christi (60 days following Easter) and All Saints' Day (November 1), which are celebrated by Catholics, and Reformation Day (October 31) and Repentance and Prayer Day (the third Wednesday in November), which are celebrated by Lutherans. In Catholic parts of Germany, there are additional holidays. All Germans celebrate Tag der Deutschen Einheit, the "Day of German Unity," on October 3. This holiday marks the 1990 reunification of East and West Germany.

The largest German festival is Oktoberfest, which takes place in Munich every fall and draws nearly 6 million people.[2] Tourists come from around the world to experience the revelry that accompanies this festival, which began in 1810 at the wedding of Crown Prince Ludwig I of Bavaria

People from all over the world visit Germany for Oktoberfest.

to Princess Therese of Sachsen-Hildburghausen. Festival-goers participate in costume parades, agricultural shows, amusement rides, music, and dancing and enjoy the many beer stands set up for the occasion.

Another large celebration, Karneval, or Carnival, takes place each year in the city of Cologne. This festival of colorful costumes, parades, and jubilant merrymaking begins on Shrove Thursday, the week before Lent, and ends a week later on Ash Wednesday, the beginning of Lent. Karneval is similar to Mardi Gras in the United States.

TRADITIONAL AND MODERN CLOTHING

Germans generally dress like people in other parts of western Europe and the United States, and young people are likely to wear casual clothing such as jeans and T-shirts. Germans might wear *Tracht*, or traditional folk clothing, during special events and festivals. Most common is the traditional dress of Bavaria, which includes lederhosen (leather stockings) for the men, along with knee socks, embroidered suspenders, and a distinctive green wool hat. For the women, traditional dress includes the dirndl, a bodice and a full, gathered skirt worn over a white blouse, with an embroidered belt and a wool hat. A cotton or linen apron, usually white, is worn over the skirt.

GERMAN FOOD

Traditional German food is hearty and heavy with meat and potatoes. The German breakfast includes rolls with butter, jam, and marmalade, plus hard- and soft-boiled eggs, yogurt, sliced meats, cheeses, juices, and coffee. Lunch is traditionally the largest meal of the day and

A traditional German meal of sausage, sauerkraut, and beer

usually consists of cooked vegetables, potatoes, and meat. The evening meal is light by American standards and may include potato salad, soup, and sausage. An even simpler evening meal, called *Abendbrot*, or "evening bread," features fruits, cold meats, and cheeses.

Germany is renowned for its wurst, or sausage. Bratwurst, *Weisswurst,* frankfurters, and braunschweiger are some of the different regional types of sausages. Before refrigeration became possible, sausage making allowed for the preservation of meat. Hundreds of different types of sausage are available across Germany.

Other common German foods include schnitzel (a breaded meat cutlet), sauerbraten (a spiced beef dish that literally means "sour meat"), *Kartoffelsalat* (a warm potato salad), sauerkraut (pickled cabbage), spaetzle (a flat noodle), and *Knoedel* (Bavarian flour dumplings). Pork and beef dishes are common traditional fare, along with vegetable soup, pickled or smoked fish and herring, pastries such as the fruit-filled strudel, and heavy, dark breads such as rye and pumpernickel.

Germany's famous Rhineland wineries produce much of the wine consumed in the country, much of which is white wine. Wines of the Mosel region are also well known. In addition, Germany is the world's third-largest producer of beer, after China and the United States. There are approximately 1,250 breweries in Germany, and together they

GUMMI BEARS

One of the world's most popular candies—the gummi bear—had its humble beginnings in Germany. Hans Riegel started his own candy company in 1920 at the age of 27 with one bag of sugar, a sheet of marble, an oven, a kettle, and a rolling pin. He made hard candies, and his wife, Gertrud, delivered them to customers in her bicycle basket. In 1922, the couple began making *Tanzbären*, or "dancing bears." These fruit-flavored gelatin candies were poured into bear-shaped molds and became an instant hit. Nearly 90 years later, gummi bears are enjoyed around the world by adults and children alike.

produce more than 5,000 brands of beer.[3] Germans consume a hefty amount of beer, averaging 32 gallons (121.4 l) a person per year.[4] Other popular beverage choices include schnapps (flavored liquor), soft drinks, coffee, and tea.

SPORTS AND LEISURE

By law, working Germans get at least 24 vacation days per year. This generous amount of vacation, combined with a relatively short workday, allows considerable time for hobbies, sports, and leisure. Jogging, swimming, volleyball, squash, gymnastics, basketball, and cycling are all common activities. Skiing is particularly popular, since Germany's mountains remain snowcapped all year.

TENNIS SUPERSTARS

In the 1980s and 1990s, German tennis players Boris Becker and Steffi Graf brought recognition to their homeland. In 1985, Becker, a native of Leimen, won the Wimbledon singles title at age 17, making him the youngest player in history to do so. In 1988, Graf, a native of Mannheim, won the Golden Slam of tennis, meaning that she won all four Grand Slams for that year—the top tennis competitions in the world. In 1999, Graf was selected as one of the best female athletes of the twentieth century. She took home 106 singles titles before retiring. She is married to US tennis great Andre Agassi.

Soccer is the most popular sport in the country. There are more than 25,000 *Fußball*, or "football," clubs across Germany, and 6.7 million members play the sport. The Deutscher Fußball-Bund, or "German Football Federation," comprises more than 170,000 teams.[5] Internationally, Germany has won three World Cups (1954, 1974, and 1990) and three European championships, making it one of the most victorious soccer teams in the world. Franz Beckenbauer is regarded a national hero. He helped his team win the 1974 World Cup and then as a coach led the Germans to victory in the 1990 World Cup.

Germany hosted soccer's FIFA World Cup in 2006.

German soccer fans cheer as their national team beats England in the 2010 World Cup.

CHAPTER 7

POLITICS: ACHIEVING UNITY

During the past century, Germany has undergone multiple changes in government and leadership. Wilhelm II ruled an empire at the beginning of the twentieth century, and the Weimar Republic followed from late 1918 to early 1933. Adolf Hitler became chancellor in 1933 and quickly established a dictatorship that lasted until the spring of 1945. Following World War II, Germany was divided in two. West Germany established a federal republic in 1949, and East Germany became a Communist state shortly thereafter. In 1982, Helmut Kohl became chancellor of West Germany, and eight years later, he reunified Germany following the fall of the Berlin Wall.

Today, the Bundesrepublik Deutschland, or Federal Republic of Germany, has a parliamentary system of democratic government. Citizens may vote at age 18. Government power is divided according to a federal system, which means that each *Länd*, or state, retains the right to handle

The German legislature convenes at the Reichstag building.

THE FLAG OF GERMANY

The official flag of the Federal Republic of Germany has three horizontal bands of equal size. From the top to the bottom, the colors are black, red, and gold. Nationalist groups used this design during the nineteenth century. At the end of the nineteenth century, after German unification, the country used a black, white, and red striped flag. The Weimar Republic adopted the black, red, and gold flag after World War I and used it until 1933, when the Nazis rose to power and replaced it with their own flag. After 1949, West Germany adopted the black, red, and gold flag, and, in 1990, it became the flag of the reunified Germany. Sometimes the German coat of arms, a black eagle on a gold shield, is included in the center of the flag.

local affairs independently. Each Länd has its own constitution, but its laws and regulations must fall within the framework of Germany's constitution, called Grundgesetz, or Basic Law.

The Basic Law was established and took effect in West Germany on May 23, 1949. Following the reunification of Germany on October 3, 1990, the Basic Law was applied to the whole country with minor amendments.

Each German Länd has its own parliament, called Ländtag, which is comprised of a minister-president and a cabinet that manages the state's affairs. Each state government is responsible for health care, education, public communication, and cultural affairs. Each state government also oversees

The flag of Germany

its own police force, makes local laws, and enforces federal laws. Each state receives a portion of the federal taxes that are collected.

STRUCTURE OF THE GOVERNMENT OF GERMANY

Executive Branch	Legislative Branch	Judicial Branch
President (head of state) Chancellor (head of government) Cabinet	Bundesrat (Federal Council) Bundestag (Federal Assembly)	Bundesverfassungsgericht (Federal Constitutional Court) Lower courts: ordinary court, labor court, administrative court, social court, fiscal court

THE EXECUTIVE AND LEGISLATIVE BRANCHES

Germany's legislative branch consists of two bodies or houses: the Bundestag and the Bundesrat. The lower house is the Bundestag, or Federal Assembly. It is comprised of a varying number of members

(622 in 2011) who are elected to four-year terms. The Bundestag elects the nation's chancellor, who makes federal policies.

The upper house is called the Bundesrat, or Federal Council. It consists of 69 members who are ministers or designated high-level officials from each state's government. Each of the 16 states can appoint between three and six members, depending on its population. This body of officials represents the interests of the states and also has veto power over legislation.

Germany's executive branch consists of the president, the chancellor, and the cabinet. The president is elected to serve a five-year term by the Bundestag and members of the state parliaments and may be reelected only once. Although considered the nation's head of state, the president plays a largely ceremonial role. He or she plays only a minor part in day-to-day governance.

POLITICAL PARTIES

Germany has five major political parties. The Christian Democratic Union (CDU) and its Bavarian sister party, the Christian Social Union (CSU), receive strong backing from Protestants and Catholics. These two parties are conservative. The Social Democratic Party (SPD) is Germany's oldest political party and historically has supported the interests of the working class. The Free Democratic Party (FDP) is a liberal party that supports human rights, civil liberties, and free enterprise. The Alliance '90/The Greens Party resulted from a merger of two separate parties and now focuses on environmental concerns, animal rights, homosexual rights, and other issues typically associated with left-wing politics.

The chancellor serves as head of the government and head of the cabinet. Unlike the president, the chancellor may be reelected an unlimited number of times. The chancellor recommends cabinet officers (called ministers), but the president must officially appoint them. The chancellor may only be dismissed before his or her term has ended by a parliamentary vote of "constructive no confidence," which means the Bundestag must vote to remove the chancellor and agree on a successor at the same time.

Christian Wulff was elected president of Germany in 2010 at the age of 51, making him Germany's youngest president ever. Angela Merkel, the country's current chancellor, was re-elected to a second term in 2009 after her initial election in 2005. Chancellor Merkel was Germany's first female chancellor. Both Wulff and Merkel are members of the Christian Democratic Union party (CDU).

German President Christian Wulff, *left*, and German Chancellor Angela Merkel, *right*

THE JUDICIAL BRANCH

The Bundesverfassungsgericht, or Federal Constitutional Court, is the country's highest court of appeal. The Bundestag and the Bundesrat each appoint half of the judges to this court. Most of the court cases heard at the federal level begin at the state level. Cases escalate to the federal court system when the issue involves more than one state or affects the entire country.

The court system is comprised of five types of lower courts. The ordinary court handles civil and criminal cases, and the labor court deals with labor relations. The administrative court hears disputes between citizens and the state, the social court handles social programs, and the fiscal court oversees tax matters.

GERMAN MILITARY

Following World War II, other European countries wanted to prevent Germany from having a powerful military again. As a result, Germany was completely demilitarized, and the Allied authorities that occupied the country forbade the reestablishment of German military forces.

In 1955, West Germany was allowed to establish the Bundeswehr, or Federal Defense Force. When Germany was reunified in 1990, the militaries of East Germany and West Germany were consolidated. Today, the Bundeswehr includes the Joint Support Service, the Central Medical Services, and an army, navy, and air force.

German Defense Minister Karl-Theodor zu Guttenberg visiting with Bundeswehr soldiers deployed in Afghanistan in 2010

More than 50 years ago, compulsory military service was instituted. All young men had to serve six months in the German military or perform alternate service. Women were allowed to serve in the medical services beginning in 1975, and in 2001, they earned the right to serve in all military branches. Even so, compulsory service was not required of women. In October 2010, Germany's leaders voted to suspend compulsory service beginning in July 2011, relying instead on a volunteer military.

CHAPTER 8

ECONOMICS: INDUSTRIAL LEADER

After Germany reunified in 1990, the country struggled with the cost of modernizing the former East Germany's industries and rebuilding its outdated infrastructure. Yet in the last two decades, Germany has solidified its position as the largest national economy in Europe, in terms of purchasing power, and the fifth-largest economy in the world.[1] Germany is part of the European Union and has used the euro as its national currency since 2002.

STRENGTH IN MANUFACTURING AND MINING

Manufacturing provides the foundation of Germany's economic strength. Close to one-third of working Germans are employed in the industrial

Euros are the currency for many countries in the European Union, including Germany.

THE EURO

Before introduction of the euro, each European country had its own currency. This made it necessary for people to exchange currencies whenever they traveled from one country to another. It also created financial risk for corporations that did business abroad, because they could not be sure of the equivalent costs in their own currencies as foreign currencies moved up and down in value. For example, before the euro, if a German company invested in a French business and the value of the French franc went down, the company had difficulty calculating the amount of the loss in German deutsche marks.

Currently, there are 17 members of the Eurozone: countries that are members of the European Union, Germany included, that agreed to exchange their old currencies for the new euro. To participate, countries were supposed to meet strict financial guidelines, including having a budget deficit of no more than 3 percent of their GDP.[4]

Germany began using the euro in January 2002. Prior to 2002, the German deutsche mark was the nation's official currency. Euro banknotes and coins feature symbols of European unity. Banknotes range from five to 500 euros, and coin denominations range from one cent to two euros.

sector.[2] Iron, steel, chemicals, and textiles are produced in the most heavily populated and industrialized region: the Ruhr River valley and surrounding Westphalia. The Ruhr valley is home to the richest coalfields in Europe. Huge refineries change iron ore into steel, which is used in some of Germany's other industries. In recent years, however, many coal mines have closed while employment in the service industries has grown.

Germany is the world's third-largest automobile manufacturer, after the United States and Japan, and it remains Europe's largest producer of automobiles.[3] Germany is home to several world-renowned

Germany manufactures several high-end automobile brands, including Mercedes, BMW, and Porsche.

A CAR FOR EVERYONE

In 2010, Germany produced more than 5.5 million automobiles and exported more than 4.2 million.[5] The nation has long been Europe's largest producer of automobiles, and its expensive, high-performance cars are popular all over the developed world.

The automobile industry has a rich history in Germany. In the 1880s, Gottlieb Daimler invented the gasoline engine in Stuttgart, Germany. Meanwhile, Karl Benz set up his own gasoline engine manufacturing company in Mannheim. In 1901, Daimler sold his very first luxury car, the Mercedes. In 1926, Daimler and Benz merged to form Mercedes-Benz, a producer of renowned luxury cars.

But perhaps the most famous German car is the Volkswagen (VW), or the so-called people's car. It was designed to be affordable for people with modest means. In 1938, the first factory was officially opened by Adolf Hitler. Production halted during World War II, but the Volkswagen Beetle entered production soon after the war was over. By 1972, the number of VW Beetles produced had surpassed that of Ford Motor Company's famous Model T.[6]

automobile companies, including Mercedes Benz, Volkswagen, Bavarian Motor Works (BMW), Audi, and Porsche. Other chief industrial products include trucks, machinery, ships, and optics. Germany also produces large quantities of cement, electric equipment, and processed foods and beverages, and it is one of the world's leading producers of wind turbines and solar power technology. The country's chemical industry turns out pharmaceuticals, fertilizers, and plastics.

Germany has deposits of lead, copper, tin, coal, nickel, uranium, and aluminum, and it is a leading producer of potash (a potassium compound) and salt. Small amounts of natural gas and petroleum are also found in Germany, but most of the nation's gas is imported from Russia and most of its oil from Russia, Norway, and the Middle East. Throughout the nineteenth century, Germany used deposits of high-quality coal to fuel its industrial growth. However, today, most of the coal that remains is of lower quality. The country is a leading producer of this material, called brown coal or lignite, but it is only useful for heating.

Resources of Germany

AGRICULTURE

Agriculture contributes less than 1 percent of Germany's gross domestic product (GDP) and employs approximately 2.4 percent of the nation's labor force.[7] Over the years, large commercial farms and cooperatives have emerged and the number of family-run farms has slowly dwindled.

Most of the smaller farms that still exist are worked by part-time farmers who also hold other jobs.

Germany has become one of the world's largest importers of agricultural goods, yet it remains a producer of barley, potatoes, rye, sugar beets, and milk. Crops vary based on the area. Along the Rhine and Mosel Rivers, grapes are grown for the production of wines. Along the northern coast, dairy farming is most common. In the foothills of the Alps, farmers raise sheep and cattle in the rich pasture lands. Farmers around the country grow apples, oats, wheat, and cabbages and raise hogs, horses, poultry, sheep, and beef and dairy cattle.

THE SERVICE INDUSTRY AND TOURISM

The largest percentage of employed Germans—nearly 70 percent— works in the service industries, which includes professions such as finance, real estate, business, teaching, and hairstyling. Germany's service industry accounts for more than 70 percent of the country's GDP.[8]

Germans working in services cater to the tens of millions of visitors who come to their country every year—the eighth most visited travel destination in the world.[9] Those employees work in hotels, restaurants, retail shops, and tourist attractions. In 2011, tourism directly employed 750,000 workers and supported jobs for 1.2 million more Germans. Including its wider economic impact, tourism accounted for 4.6 percent of the GDP.[10]

Germany's rich land is good for raising sheep.

GERMANY'S INFRASTRUCTURE

Germany has a highly developed system of transportation. It has had railroads since 1838, when the first track connected Berlin and Potsdam. Since then, the German railway system has become one of the most extensive rail networks worldwide. Deutsche Bahn AG, the country's national railroad and Europe's largest railway operator, transports 1.9 billion passengers every year, or approximately 5 million passengers every day, along with 857,000 short tons (777,457 metric tons) of freight daily.[11]

In 1933, Adolf Hitler began construction of Germany's famed Bundesautobahnen, known in English as the autobahn, a system of superhighways

MASS COMMUNICATION

Germany boasts hundreds of daily newspapers. The German press is not censored by the government, except Nazi propaganda is strictly forbidden. Germany's largest newspaper, *Bild* (Picture) is published in Hamburg, and another major daily paper, *Die Welt* (The World) is based in Berlin. Other important newspapers include the *Frankfurter Allgemeine Zeitung*, which is published in Frankfurt am Main, and *Sueddeutsche Zeitung*, produced in Munich. The weekly publication *Die Zeit* (The Time) appeals to people of the academic class.

Germany has public and private radio and television broadcasting corporations. Public channels run only limited commercials. Purchasers of televisions and radios pay a license fee that provides funding for public broadcasting. Private broadcasting companies sell advertising to finance their operations.

The autobahn

that crisscross the country. The autobahn system includes more than 7,000 miles (11,265 km) of highways, many of which have no speed limit.[12] Germans have a high rate of private automobile ownership and many enjoy being able to drive fast without restrictions.

Lufthansa, Germany's national airline, provides daily flights to and from cities throughout the world. Germany's largest international airports are located in Frankfurt am Main, Munich, Düsseldorf, Berlin, and Hamburg. Germany's chief seaports are located in Bremerhaven, Hamburg, and Wilhelmshaven.

UNEMPLOYMENT AND POVERTY

Germany has long since recovered economically from World War II. In 2008, Germany's unemployment rate dropped to 7.8 percent, the lowest rate since reunification in 1990.[13] Unemployment increased slightly during the recession of 2008 and 2009, but the economy bounced back smartly during 2010 with healthy manufacturing growth.

Germany's estimated 2010 GDP per capita, defined as the value of the total goods and services produced divided by the country's population, was $35,990. This put the country in thirty-first place in the world and marked a 3.4 percent rise from the previous year. Even so, in 2010, 15.5 percent of Germans lived below the poverty line.[14]

One of Germany's greatest economic challenges is rooted in the continued need for modernization in the former East Germany, especially its manufacturing industry. Having an adequate workforce of skilled laborers is viewed as a long-term problem, given the low fertility rate among native Germans. With the average couple having no more than one child, the country's future workforce will decrease and the burden of supporting a larger number of retired people will increase. However, in the hope of improving economic efficiency, the German government continues to support structural reforms, including some targeted tax cuts and subsidies.

RECOVERING FROM WORLD WAR II

At the end of World War II, Germany lay in ruins. Its infrastructure of streets, bridges, utilities, and buildings was severely damaged. As the German people struggled to put their lives back together, many feared that the years following World War II would echo the problems that followed World War I, including high levels of inflation and unemployment.

The western Allies eventually came to realize that Germany would need assistance to stabilize its currency, rebuild its infrastructure, and rejuvenate its economy. Beginning in 1948, the United States instituted the Marshall Plan, which provided economic aid to Western European countries in the hope that prosperity would help them resist communism. Coupled with the German people's fierce determination to rebuild their economy, the plan proved successful in West Germany. In the early 1950s, the nation's economy blossomed. This recovery is often called the *Wirtschaftswunder*, or "economic miracle." East Germany struggled economically, but because of its highly skilled labor force, it fared better than other Communist countries in Eastern Europe.

CHAPTER 9
GERMANY TODAY

Daily life in Germany is similar to that in the United States. Families are typically nuclear, which means that most households consist of parents and their children but not older generations or extended families. Often, both parents work in order to afford a high standard of living.

Germans have traded some of their traditional customs for a more modern lifestyle. Fast-food restaurants and US television programs have become common, and cell phones, MP3 players, and laptops have come into wide use, especially by young people. In large cities, people enjoy attending nightclubs and concerts.

Most Germans in the labor force work only a 35-hour workweek, and the law requires that they have at least 24 days of vacation per year. When not in school or at work, Germans relax by reading, watching television, participating in sports, gardening, hiking, and engaging in a myriad of other pastimes. Germans also love to go on vacation. Their

German households usually consist of nuclear families.

most popular spots are seaside destinations in the north, but they also travel throughout the world. German citizens and foreign tourists alike enjoy the many museums, concert halls, cultural exhibits, and seasonal festivals that are subsidized by the federal government.

HOME OWNERSHIP

Nearly 60 percent of Germans rent their homes or apartments, rather than own them, giving Germany the lowest rate of home ownership in the European Union.[2] Several reasons explain this trend. One reason is that individuals with limited financial resources often find it difficult to secure a mortgage. In addition, Germany has a high standard of social housing and rental properties, so it is cheap to rent high-quality homes. The modest number of homeowners in Germany played an important role in the recession of 2008 and 2009, when housing values declined drastically worldwide. Germany was not as negatively affected as the United States and was therefore able to make a quicker financial recovery.

EDUCATION

Germans value education and place a high importance on doing well in school. The country's literacy rate is 99 percent.[1] However, the state-funded education system in Germany differs somewhat from that of US schools.

The normal school year in Germany runs for approximately ten months and includes a six-week summer break and several smaller breaks at Christmas and other times. Younger German children attend school only in the mornings (and often Saturday mornings as well), returning home by lunchtime. They

During their long vacations, some Germans travel throughout the country or abroad.

have a large amount of homework, which they complete in the afternoon. Unlike US schools, German schools do not have extensive programs of extracurricular activities and sports.

Another difference between US and German schools concerns planning for the future. In the United States, all children follow the same educational program through senior high school and then decide whether to enter the workforce or to attend a college or a vocational school. In Germany, there is a three-level educational system. Students and their parents must decide early on what level to enter, which determines their future career track. The German education system is slowly becoming more flexible, however.

Parents have the choice of sending their child to *Kindergarten*, or preschool, from ages three to six. But from ages six to 15, all German children must attend school. Children spend four years in the *Grundschule*, or primary school, where they all study the same subjects. After completing fourth grade, they are streamed into one of the three different tracks, depending on their academic ability, their teachers' recommendations, and their parents' wishes.

The German word *Kindergarten* was first used to describe a school for young children in 1837.

The first option is the *Hauptschule*, which, in most German states, consists of grades five through nine. Students

Germany has a high rate of school attendance.

in this track take courses in mathematics, physics or chemistry, biology, geography, history, music, art, religion, politics, sports, and language. However, these students are taught subjects at a slower pace, along with courses intended to teach them a vocation and prepare them for the working world. Eventually, these children go on to study at a *Berufsschule*, a vocational school, while completing an apprenticeship. These students are generally finished with their education by age 18, and they may then take a job in mechanics, construction, or a similar trade.

Another option is the *Realschule*. Students in this track attend an additional year, through grade ten. In addition to the subjects covered in a Hauptschule, students at a Realschule receive instruction to prepare them for part-time and higher vocational

PROS AND CONS OF THE GERMAN EDUCATION SYSTEM

For years, many Germans have argued that the nation's education system is unfair because it pigeonholes students too early, based on the academic performance they have demonstrated before age ten. According to this system, a student's dreams of attending university and becoming a teacher or doctor can be swiftly dashed if his or her elementary school grades are not high enough.

Others argue that this strict system keeps German children focused on their schoolwork and gives them a practical education based on their proven abilities. As one German teacher explained, "If the child is not suited to the Gymnasium, if he cannot learn foreign languages and is not good at abstract thought, then this child will continually fail and will . . . experience frustration. . . . As a result, we say, do not send children to the Gymnasium who are not suited for it. Such children belong as soon as possible in the correct educational path."[3]

schools called *Berufsfachschulen*. Completion of the Realschule option is most similar to receiving a high school diploma in the United States. Students who complete their education in the Realschule are qualified to hold jobs requiring a bit more knowledge and skill, such as office jobs.

Students with the highest grades can enroll in the third and highest level of postelementary school, the Gymnasium. The purpose of this educational track is to prepare students to enter a university. In most German states, Gymnasiums run from grade five to grade 13. Students study the same subjects as their peers in the Hauptschule and Realschule but more intensively; also, courses in Latin and Greek are added. The Gymnasium has four main courses of study, and students often focus on one of the following: humanities, modern languages, mathematics and science, or economics and social sciences. After completing their coursework, Gymnasium students take final exams and qualify for enrollment at a university.

GERMANY'S OLDEST EDUCATIONAL INSTITUTION

The University of Heidelberg, established in 1386, is Germany's oldest university. Located in Heidelberg, a city in Baden-Württemberg, the university originally offered courses in four subjects: theology, philosophy, law, and medicine.

Throughout the centuries, the University of Heidelberg has undergone several transformations. Initially established as a Catholic institution by the pope, the university became a Calvinist institution following the Reformation. However, it was later operated by the Jesuits, a Catholic order of religious men. Today, the University of Heidelberg rates as one of Europe's top-ranking universities.

Germany has more than 370 classical universities, along with technical universities, art and music colleges, and other specialized schools.[4] Students attend technical universities for four and a half years and classical universities for six and a half years. German residents attending a college or university in Germany pay little or no tuition.

CURRENT AND FUTURE CHALLENGES

Even though Germany's economy and industry are stronger than those of many of its neighbors, the country faces the challenges of prosperity. For many years into the future, Germany will have to combat air pollution from industry and environmental damage to its waterways. While clean-up efforts have increased, the problem will continue to require attention.

Additionally, Germany struggles with the difficulties of integrating and assimilating its immigrants. Some Germans object to the increase in minorities entering the country and worry about the financial burden that providing social services for these people places on the nation's taxpayers. Who will bear the cost of completing the modernization of the former East Germany continues to be an issue as well.

Despite these anticipated future hurdles, Germany has seemingly overcome the political turmoil of its controversial past. Some of the world's most brilliant minds were shaped in Germany—Beethoven,

Students relax outside the Academy of Fine Arts in Munich, one of Germany's many colleges.

GERMAN SCIENTISTS AND THE NOBEL PRIZE

To date, 80 Germans have received a Nobel Prize, 68 of whom were recognized for advancements in physics, chemistry, physiology, and medicine. The first Nobel Prize in Physics was awarded to Wilhelm Conrad Röntgen for his discovery of the X-ray in 1901. The same year, Emil von Behring won the Nobel Prize in Medicine for developing a treatment for diphtheria. Max Planck, Nobel Prize laureate in 1918 for physics, discovered energy quanta. In 1921, German-born Albert Einstein won the prize in physics for his explanation of the photoelectric effect.

Wagner, and Einstein, among others. Yet Germany has also served as the arena for some of history's darkest deeds, such as Hitler's aggression and the World War II Holocaust against the Jews. Regardless, Germany stands as an example of the possibilities that come from perseverance. This once-divided country has become whole again and plays a pivotal role in European trade and the success of the European Union.

The Brandenburg Gate in Berlin serves as a reminder of a once-divided country and a symbol of the perseverance of the German people.

TIMELINE

1700–450 BCE	Germanic tribes of people move into the area that will become Germany.
9 CE	Forces led by Hermann defeat the Romans at the Battle of the Teutoburg Forest.
98 CE	Roman historian Tacitus writes the first account of the German people, *The Germania*.
814	Emperor Charlemagne of the Holy Roman Empire dies.
1273	The Hapsburg dynasty comes to power in Germany.
1517	Martin Luther challenges the teachings of the Catholic Church and sets off the Protestant Reformation.
1618–1648	The Thirty Years' War is fought.
1862	Otto von Bismarck is appointed minister-president of Prussia by King William I.
1871	On January 18, Wilhelm I becomes Germany's first kaiser.
1914	On June 28, 1914, Archduke Franz Ferdinand of Austria-Hungary and his wife are assassinated, initiating World War I.
1919	On June 28, the Treaty of Versailles is signed, officially ending World War I.
1933	On January 30, Adolf Hitler is appointed chancellor of Germany.

1936	Germany hosts the Olympic Winter Games in the Alpine village of Garmisch-Partenkirchen.
1938	Nazi youth groups and special police smash the windows of Jewish shops and synagogues on the night of November 9, *Kristallnacht.*
1939	After Hitler's troops invade Poland on September 1, France and the United Kingdom declare war on Germany two days later.
1945	Hitler commits suicide on April 30, and Germany surrenders to Allied troops on May 7.
1949	Germany is split into West Germany and East Germany.
1961	The Berlin Wall is built, dividing East and West Berlin.
1972	Munich hosts the 1972 Olympic Summer Games.
1989	On November 9, the Berlin Wall is opened and rejoicing Germans tear it down.
1990	On October 3, East Germany and West Germany are reunited as one country.
1992	Germany signs the Maastricht Treaty, joining other nations in creating the European Union.
2002	On January 1, the euro replaces the deutsche mark as Germany's official currency.
2005	Angela Merkel becomes the first female chancellor of Germany; she is reelected in 2009.

FACTS AT YOUR FINGERTIPS

GEOGRAPHY

Official name: Federal Republic of Germany (in German, Bundesrepublik Deutschland)

Area: 137,847 square miles (357,022 sq km)

Climate: Temperate

Highest elevation: Zugspitze, 9,721 feet (2,963 m) above sea level

Lowest elevation: Neuendorf bei Wilste, 11.6 feet (3.54 m) below sea level

Significant geographic features: Rhine River, the Alps

PEOPLE

Population (July 2011 est.): 81,471,834

Most populous city: Berlin

Ethnic groups: German, 91.5 percent; Turkish, 2.4 percent; other, 6.1 percent (includes Greek, Italian, Polish, Russian, Serbo-Croatian, Spanish)

Percentage of residents living in urban areas: 74 percent

Life expectancy: 80.07 years at birth (world rank: 27)

Language: German

Religion(s): Protestantism, 34 percent; Roman Catholicism, 34 percent; Islam, 3.7 percent; unaffiliated or other, 28.3 percent

GOVERNMENT AND ECONOMY

Government: federal republic

Capital: Berlin

Date of adoption of current constitution: May 23, 1949; adopted by the united Germany on October 3, 1990

Head of state: president

Head of government: chancellor

Legislature: Bundesrat (upper house) and Bundestag (lower house)

Currency: euro

Industries and natural resources: coal, lead, copper, tin, coal, nickel, uranium, aluminum, automobile manufacturing, steel, cement, chemicals, machinery, electronics, shipbuilding, foodstuffs, textiles

NATIONAL SYMBOLS

Holidays: Germans celebrate ten official holidays: New Year's Day, Good Friday, Easter Monday, Labor Day (May 1), Ascension Day, Whit Monday, Day of German Unity

(October 3), Reformation Day (October 31), Christmas Day (December 25), and Saint Stephen's Day (December 26).

Flag: Three horizontal bands of black, red, and gold

National anthem: "Lied der Deutschen" ("Song of the Germans"); only the third verse is sung because the other verses are associated with the Nazi Party.

Coat of arms: A black eagle on a gold shield

KEY PEOPLE

Johann Sebastian Bach (1685–1750), wrote more than 1,000 pieces of music and is considered one of the greatest composers in history

Martin Luther (1483–1546), monk, professor, and theologian who sparked the Protestant Reformation against the Catholic Church

Otto von Bismarck (1815–1898), founder and first chancellor of the German Empire

Adolf Hitler (1889–1945), leader of the Nazi Party and führer of Germany from 1933–1945; led Germany during World War II and was responsible for initiating the Holocaust

Helmut Kohl (1930–),chancellor of West Germany from 1982–1990 and the unified Germany from 1990–1998; campaigned vigorously for German reunification

STATE; CAPITAL

Baden-Württemberg; Stuttgart

Bavaria (Bayern); Munich

Berlin—the city of Berlin is its own state

Brandenburg; Potsdam

Bremen—the city of Bremen is its own state

Hamburg—the city of Hamburg is its own state

Hesse (Hessen); Wiesbaden

Mecklenburg–Western Pomerania (Mecklenburg-Vorpommern); Schwerin

Lower Saxony (Niedersachsen); Hanover

North Rhine–Westphalia (Nordrhein-Westfalen); Düsseldorf

Rhineland-Palatinate (Rheinland-Pfalz); Mainz

Saarland; Saarbrücken

Saxony (Sachsen); Dresden

Saxony-Anhalt (Sachsen-Anhalt); Magdeburg

Schleswig-Holstein; Kiel

Thuringia (Thüringen); Erfurt

*German spelling given in parentheses if different from English

GLOSSARY

chancellor

The chief minister of a state or country.

concentration camp

A camp where prisoners are held.

dissenter

A person who disagrees.

duchy

A territory ruled by a duke.

dynasty

A succession of rulers from the same family.

escarpment

A steep cliff or slope in front of a fortress.

excommunicate

To force someone out of the Roman Catholic Church.

foehn

A warm, dry wind that blows down the side of a mountain.

Gastarbeiter

"Guest worker"; a migrant worker who moves to Germany in search of employment.

heathlands

A habitat of low-growing vegetation on infertile soil.

propaganda

The spreading of information, rumors, or ideas with the intent to harm or benefit a specific organization, person, or cause.

reparations

Payments made by a defeated country to make amends for destruction caused during a war.

ADDITIONAL RESOURCES

SELECTED BIBLIOGRAPHY

Ivory, Michael. *Germany.* Washington, DC: National Geographic, 2010. Print.

Sandford, John, ed. *Encyclopedia of Contemporary German Culture*. New York: Routledge, 2001. Print.

Schulze, Hagen. *Germany: A New History*. Cambridge, MA: Harvard UP, 2001. Print.

FURTHER READINGS

Ayer, Eleanor H. *Germany*. San Diego, CA: Lucent, 1999. Print.

Fuller, Barbara, and Gabriele Vossmeyer. *Germany.* Tarrytown, NY: Benchmark, 2004. Print.

WEB LINKS

To learn more about Germany, visit ABDO Publishing Company online at **www.abdopublishing.com**. Web sites about Germany are featured on our Book Links page. These links are routinely monitored and updated to provide the most current information available.

PLACES TO VISIT

If you are ever in Germany, consider checking out these important and interesting sites!

Berlin Wall Memorial

The Berlin Wall Memorial commemorates those Germans who lived behind the wall and those who lost their lives trying to cross into freedom.

Dachau Concentration Camp

Dachau is the site of the first concentration camp opened in Germany during World War II. The tour gives visitors a grim and realistic view of the horrors faced by the 200,000 humans imprisoned there from 1933 to 1945.

Neuschwanstein and Hohenschwangau Castles

These breathtaking castles in Bavaria are among the most popular tourist destinations in Europe.

Zugspitze

Visitors can take a train partway up the mountain and then travel to the Zugspitze, Germany's highest Alpine peak, by cogwheel train or cable car.

SOURCE NOTES

CHAPTER 1. A VISIT TO GERMANY

1. "Munich 1972 Olympic Games." *Encyclopædia Britannica*. Encyclopædia Britannica, 2011. Web. 30 Jan. 2011.

CHAPTER 2. GEOGRAPHY: SCENIC BEAUTY

1. "Alps." *Encyclopædia Britannica*. Encyclopædia Britannica, 2011. Web. 30 Jan. 2011.

2. "Zugspitze." *Encyclopædia Britannica*. Encyclopædia Britannica, 2011. Web. 30 Jan. 2011.

3. "The World Factbook: Germany." *Central Intelligence Agency*. Central Intelligence Agency, 16 Mar. 2011. Web. 25 Mar. 2011.

4. Joseph Gonzalez and Thomas E. Sherer Jr. *The Complete Idiot's Guide to Geography*. New York: Penguin, 2004. Print. 107.

5. James J. Sheehan. "Germany." *World Book Advanced*. World Book, 2011. Web. 12 Apr. 2011.

6. "Rhine River." *Encyclopædia Britannica*. Encyclopædia Britannica, 2011. Web. 30 Jan. 2011.

7. "Brocken." *Encyclopædia Britannica*. Encyclopædia Britannica, 2011. Web. 30 Jan. 2011.

8. James J. Sheehan. "Germany." *World Book Advanced*. World Book, 2011. Web. 12 Apr. 2011.

9. John W. Boyer. "Lorelei." *World Book Advanced*. World Book, 2011. Web. 12 Apr. 2011.

10. James J. Sheehan. "Germany." *World Book Advanced*. World Book, 2011. Web. 12 Apr. 2011.

11. "Lake Constance." *Encyclopædia Britannica*. Encyclopædia Britannica, 2011. Web. 30 Jan. 2011.

12. James J. Sheehan. "Germany." *World Book Advanced*. World Book, 2011. Web. 12 Apr. 2011.

13. "Country Guide: Germany." *BBC: Weather*. BBC, n.d. Web. 14 Jan. 2011.

CHAPTER 3. ANIMALS AND NATURE: CREATURES OF THE FOREST

1. Regina Friedrich. "Wolves in Germany." *Experiencing Germany: Goethe-Institut*. Goethe-Institut, Feb. 2010. Web. 3 Jan. 2011.

2. "Biosphere Reserve Information: Germany, Schaalsee." *MAB Programme: UNESCO—MAB Biosphere Reserves Directory*. UNESCO, 28 Feb. 2007. Web. 13 Apr. 2011.

3. "Land Use." *Federal Statistical Office and the Statistical Offices of the Länder*. Federal Statistical Office and the Statistical Offices of the Länder, 20 May 2010. Web. 26 Dec. 2010.

4. "Summary Statistics: Summaries by Country, Table 5, Threatened Species in Each Country." *IUCN Red List of Threatened Species*. International Union for Conservation of Nature and Natural Resources, 2010. Web. 24 Mar. 2011.

5. "German National Parks." *Official Tourism Web Site of Germany*. German National Tourist Board, n.d. Web. 26 Dec. 2010.

CHAPTER 4. HISTORY: AN IMPERIAL PAST

1. Charles W. Eliot, ed. *Voyages and Travels: Ancient and Modern*. New York: Collier, 1910. *Google Book Search*. Web. 13 Apr. 2011.

2. "The Great War: WWI Casualty and Death Tables." *PBS Online*. PBS, n.d. Web. 10 Apr. 2011.

3. "Germany." *Encyclopædia Britannica*. Encyclopædia Britannica, 2011. Web. 30 Jan. 2011.

4. "German Jews during the Holocaust: 1939–1945." *Holocaust Encyclopedia*. United States Holocaust Memorial Museum, 6 Jan. 2011. Web. 13 Apr. 2011.

5. "Introduction to the Holocaust." *Holocaust Encyclopedia*. United States Holocaust Memorial Museum, 6 Jan. 2011. Web. 13 Apr. 2011.

6. "Berlin Wall." *Encyclopædia Britannica*. Encyclopædia Britannica, 2011. Web. 30 Jan. 2011.

7. James J. Sheehan. "Berlin Airlift." *World Book Advanced*. World Book, 2011. Web. 8 Apr. 2011.

8. "Berlin Blockade and Airlift." *Encyclopædia Britannica*. Encyclopædia Britannica, 2011. Web. 30 Jan. 2011.

9. "Fatalities at the Berlin Wall: 1961–1989." *Berlin Wall Memorial*. Berlin Wall Memorial, 2011. Web 14 Apr. 2011.

10. Steven Kinzer. "Evolution in Europe; Kohl Is Savoring 'This Happy Hour.'" *New York Times*. New York Times, 25 Nov. 1990. Web. 6 Jan. 2011.

CHAPTER 5. PEOPLE: NATIONAL PRIDE

1. "The World Factbook: Germany." *Central Intelligence Agency*. Central Intelligence Agency, 16 Mar. 2011. Web. 25 Mar. 2011.

2. Ibid.

3. Ibid.

4. Ibid.

5. Ibid.

6. Ibid.

7. Ibid.

8. Ibid.

9. Ibid.

10. "Turkey in the EU: What the Public Thinks." *EurActiv.com.* EurActiv Network, 20 Aug. 2009. Web. 12 Feb. 2011.

11. "The World Factbook: Germany." *Central Intelligence Agency.* Central Intelligence Agency, 16 Mar. 2011. Web. 25 Mar. 2011.

12. Ibid.

13. Ibid.

14. "Introduction to the Holocaust." *Holocaust Encyclopedia.* United States Holocaust Memorial Museum, 6 Jan. 2011. Web. 13 Apr. 2011.

15. Rami Tal. "The Jewish People Policy Planning Institute Annual Assessment 2009." *Jewish People Policy Institute.* Jewish People Policy Institute, 2009. Web. 13 Apr. 2011.

16. "Quelling the Flight from the Church (Tax)." *Deutsche Welle.* Deutsche Welle, 13 Apr. 2004. Web. 5 May 2011.

CHAPTER 6. CULTURE: A CLASSICAL TRADITION

1. "Why Germany, Why Germany?" *DAAD: German Academic Exchange Service.* DAAD: German Academic Exchange Service, n.d. Web. 12 Jan. 2011.

2. "Munich Germany." *Germany-Explorer.com.* Germany-Explorer.com, n.d. Web. 20 Jan. 2011.

3. "German Breweries." *German Beer Institute.* German Beer Institute, n.d. Web. 2 Feb. 2011.

4. "Brewers Not Worried by Beer Consumption Drop." *Deutsche Welle.* Deutsche Welle, 23 Apr. 2010. Web. 6 Jan. 2011.

5. "Profile: Members." *Deutscher Fussball-Bund.* DFB, 6 Apr. 2011. Web. 13 Apr. 2011.

CHAPTER 7. POLITICS: ACHIEVING UNITY

None.

CHAPTER 8. ECONOMICS: INDUSTRIAL LEADER

1. "The World Factbook: Germany." *Central Intelligence Agency.* Central Intelligence Agency, 16 Mar. 2011. Web. 25 Mar. 2011.

2. Ibid.

3. "Country Profiles: Germany." *ACEA: European Automobile Manufacturers' Association.* ACEA, 2011. Web. 25 Apr. 2011.

4. "European Union." *Encyclopædia Britannica.* Encyclopædia Britannica, 2011. Web. 30 Jan. 2011.

5. "Germany's Passenger Car Production up 12 Percent in 2010." *Steel Orbis*. Steel Orbis Electronic Marketplace, 7 Jan. 2011. Web. 14 Apr. 2011.

6. "This Day in Tech: Feb. 17, 1972: Beetle Outruns Model T." *Wired*. Condé Nast, 17 Feb. 2010. Web. 14 Apr. 2011.

7. "The World Factbook: Germany." *Central Intelligence Agency*. Central Intelligence Agency, 16 Mar. 2011. Web. 25 Mar. 2011.

8. Ibid.

9. "UNWTO Tourism Highlights: 2010 Edition." *United Nations World Tourism Organization*. United Nations World Tourism Organization, 2010. Web. 5 May 2011.

10. "Germany: Key Facts at a Glance." *World Travel and Tourism Council*. World Travel and Tourism Council, 2011. Web. 5 May 2011.

11. "Deutsche Bahn at a Glance." *Deutsche Bahn*. Deutsche Bahn, n.d. Web. 10 Jan. 2011.

12. "Autobahn." *Encyclopædia Britannica*. Encyclopædia Britannica, 2011. Web. 30 Jan. 2011.

13. "The World Factbook: Germany." *Central Intelligence Agency*. Central Intelligence Agency, 16 Mar. 2011. Web. 25 Mar. 2011.

14. Ibid.

CHAPTER 9. GERMANY TODAY

1. "The World Factbook: Germany." *Central Intelligence Agency*. Central Intelligence Agency, 16 Mar. 2011. Web. 25 Mar. 2011.

2. "A Rental Nation? Germans Looking to Buy Those Four Walls." *Deutsche Welle*. Deutsche Welle, 9 May 2006. Web. 2 Jan. 2011.

3. Diana Kendall. *Sociology in Our Times*. Belmont, CA: Thomson Wadworth, 2008. *Google Book Search*. Web. 13 Apr. 2011.

4. "Education and Research." *Facts about Germany*. Facts about Germany, n.d. Web. 8 Apr. 2011.

[INDEX]

Alps, 10–13, 17, 19–21,
24–27, 34, 110
animals, 29–34, 38
architecture, 85
area, 15, 18
arts, 21, 82, 84–86, 122, 125
autobahn, 112–114
automobiles, 36, 106–108,
114

Bach, Johann Sebastian,
77–78
Baltic Sea, 18–19, 24, 26, 34
Basic Law, 73, 96
Bavaria, 7, 8, 10, 13, 17, 18, 24,
26, 27, 34, 41, 68, 82, 86, 88,
90, 100, 108
beer, 7, 21, 88, 90–91
Beethoven, Ludwig van, 78,
125
Berlin, 15, 18, 23, 26–27,
60–62, 70, 71, 74, 80, 112,
114
Berlin Wall, 62, 95
Bismarck, Otto von, 47–48
Black Forest, 20, 23–24, 34
boar, 29–32
bordering countries, 18

Catholicism, 46, 73–74, 86,
100, 123
Celts, 43
Charlemagne, 46
cinema, 83–86

climate, 24–27
clothing, 88
coat of arms, 29, 96
Cold War, 60
Cologne, 23, 71, 74, 88
communism, 14, 55, 58–60,
62, 95, 115
constitution, 51, 73, 96, 98,
102
currency, 15, 51, 52, 60, 61,
64, 105, 106, 115

Danube River, 23–24, 44
deutsche mark, 64, 106
Dietrich, Marlene, 84
Dürer, Albrecht, 85

East Germany, 14, 60–63, 74,
95, 102, 105, 115, 125
economic growth, 60, 61, 105,
109
education, 96, 118–125
Einstein, Albert, 126
Elbe River, 23
endangered species, 38
environmental threats, 36–41,
100, 125
ethnic groups, 43, 55, 69, 73
euro, 15, 64, 105, 106
European Union, 105, 118,
126
exports, 106–109
Expressionism, 83, 86

food, 10, 32, 61, 88–91, 108,
117
France, 14, 17–18, 19, 44–51,
56, 60, 67
Frankfurt, 26, 82, 112–114
Füssen, 10–13

Germanic peoples, 43–46,
55, 68
Goebbels, Joseph, 55
Goethe, Johann Wolfgang
von, 82
government structure, 14, 15,
47, 60–62, 95–103
Grimm, Jacob and Wilhelm,
83
gross domestic product, 15,
106, 108–110, 114

Hamburg, 18, 23, 26, 41, 71,
112, 114
Handel, George Frideric,
77–78
Hapsburg dynasty, 46–47
Harz Mountains, 21, 41
Hermann, 43
Hitler, Adolf, 52, 95, 108, 112
Hohenstaufen dynasty, 46
holidays, 86–88
Holocaust, 58, 74, 126

immigration, 68–69, 70, 74, 125

imports, 109–110

industries, 38, 105–110

infrastructure, 61, 105, 112–115

Islam, 74

Italy, 17–18, 44–46, 48, 56, 69, 70

Jewish people, 55, 58, 74, 126

Judaism, 74

Kohl, Helmut, 62, 63, 95

Lang, Fritz, 83

language, 15, 44, 72–73, 80, 122–123

leaders, current 15, 60, 63, 101, 103

life expectancy, 70

literacy rate, 118

literature, 82–83

Mendelssohn, Felix, 78

Merkel, Angela, 101

military, 8, 48, 102–103

Mosel River, 19, 90, 110

Munich, 7–10, 23, 71, 86, 112, 114

music, 77–80, 86–88, 122, 125

national capital, 15

national parks, 23, 41

natural resources, 41, 109

Nazi Party, 8, 52–55, 58, 63, 69, 80, 84, 96, 112

Neuschwanstein Castle, 13

Nobel Prize, 83, 126

North Central Plain, 19, 26, 34, 36

North Sea, 18, 19, 23–24, 38

official name, 15

Oktoberfest, 86

Olympic Games, 8, 24

oompah band, 7, 86

Petersen, Wolfgang, 84

plants, 34–41

political parties, 100

polka, 86

population, 15, 67–71

poverty, 114–115

Protestantism, 46

Prussia, 47

religion, 15, 46, 73–74, 122

Rhine River, 19, 21, 23, 38–39, 44, 110

Riefenstahl, Leni, 84

Romans, 43–44

Russia, 27, 48, 67, 69, 74, 109
   See also Soviet Union

sausage, 89–90

Schumann, Robert, 78

Soviet Union, 14, 32, 56–62,
   See also Russia

sports, 17, 91–92, 117, 121–122

teenage life, 80, 122–123

tourism, 24, 110

Turkey, 69–70

United Kingdom, 14, 48, 56, 60, 80

United Nations, 39

United States, 14, 24, 51, 56, 60–61, 67, 80, 84, 88, 90, 115, 117, 118, 121, 123

universities, 123–125

Wagner, Richard, 13, 78, 126

Weimar Republic, 51–52, 95–96

West Germany, 8, 14, 60–64, 70, 86, 95–96, 102, 115

William I, 47

wine, 90, 110

wolves, 31

World War I, 48, 51, 83, 96, 115,

World War II, 14, 31, 36, 55–62, 74, 80, 82, 83, 95, 102, 108, 114, 115, 126

Wulff, Christian, 101

Zugspitze, 17, 24

PHOTO CREDITS